Is The Virgin Mary Appearing At Medjugorje?

An urgent message for the world given in a Marxist country

René Laurentin/Ljudevit Rupčić

Translated by
Francis Martin

The Word Among Us Press
P.O. Box 3646
Washington, D.C. 20037

Acknowledgements

Scripture quotations in this publication are taken from The Holy Bible, New International Version, Copyright © 1973, 1978, International Bible Society.

Photographs by:

James Appleman, p. 66
All remaining photographs taken by René Laurentin and Stan and Marge Karminski.

The Word Among Us Press
P.O. Box 3646
Washington, D.C. 20037

I dedicate this book to St. Bernadette of Lourdes. May she render fraternal assistance, within the Communion of Saints, to her Croatian brothers and sisters in Medjugorje. Like her, their only goal is to respond fully to love.

They remind us of Bernadette, despite the differences in time, place, ethnic background, languages, culture, and health. As Gather Cros said of Bernadette in 1865, "I wish you could see the simplicity, the utter simplicity, the simplicity with dignity, that nature cannot counterfeit."

Like Bernadette on the second day, they sprinkled holy water at the apparition. Like her, they received a message of prayer and conversion aimed at a sinful world that has become deaf to the message of the Gospel.

Is The Virgin Mary Appearing At Medjugorje?

Table of Contents

AUSTRIA
HUNGARY
SLOVENIA
Ljubljana
Zagreb
Trieste
CROATIA
Rijeka
ROMANIA
VOJVODINA
Novi Sad
Sava
Danube
BOSNIA
HERCEGOVINA
BELGRADE
Drina
Sarajevo
ADRIATIC
Split
Citluk
Mostar
SERBIA
Morava
MONTENEGRO
Pristina
Titograd
KOSOVO
Dubrovnik
ALBANIA
Skopie
Vardar
BULGARIA
MACEDONIA
SEA
ITALY
GREECE
MEDITERRANEAN
SEA
MOSTAR
Citluk
Ljubuski
MEDJUGORJE
Neretva
Capljina
Metkovic

Introduction

THE APPARITIONS AT MEDJUGORJE BEGAN ON JUNE 24, 1981. In Yugoslavia, especially in the region of Hercegovina, their impact was just as dramatic as that of Lourdes in 1858. The repercussion among theologians was worldwide. Articles and publications multiplied to the point where the Western world could no longer ignore Medjugorje.

At the present stage of events, the local ordinary, Bishop Pavao Žanić, who has responsibility for rendering judgment in such matters, is cautioning against any hasty action and all "irresponsible propaganda." He recommends that serious attention be given to every objection and difficulty. This book has faithfully followed his directives, which are, moreover, most useful in bringing the whole truth to light.

This book is a work of research. The disadvantage of requesting an *Imprimatur* is that it would have seemed to approve of the apparitions well ahead of the judgment of the responsible bishop. This view was shared by the bishops responsible for Christian publications in France. This book is therefore being published in accordance with the norms governing any research, and is the sole responsibility of the author.

At the time of writing, in January 1984, and when preparing the latest edition in September 1984 (represented by this English translation), the apparitions are still going on in Medjugorje. One of the girls no longer sees the apparitions: a harbinger of their impending end. According to the messages already received, the end of the apparitions will be marked by a visible and permanent sign. The sign will be left on the mountain for all unbelievers to see. The message received in Medjugorje is a serious warning from heaven to a world bent on self-destruction. It was accepted with uncommon openness and conviction by the parishioners there and by the two million

1

visitors who have visited Medjugorje. The message is an appeal to prayer, conversion, and fasting, in order to change our world of violence. As such, it is a pure echo of the Gospel.

As a theologian I was aware of the paradox of my situation while composing this work because of two conflicting demands. First, at Medjugorje the Virgin is calling people to believe without waiting for tomorrow; tomorrow will be too late. Second, Church authority is urging that there be prior verification in order to be sure that it is the Virgin who is speaking.

This is what usually happens with prophetic messages. More often than not, prophets have been believed after their death rather than during their lifetime; and by then it was too late. It therefore seemed appropriate that two books on Medjugorje appear simultaneously. They complement one another. The book by Philippe Madre (see bibliography) deals with faith and hope, in the spirit of the Gospel maxim that "He who puts his hand to the plow and looks back is not worthy of the kingdom." My own work, on the other hand, has tried to be sensitive to all the aspects of the event. I have tried to take into account objections and difficulties in order to facilitate a balanced evaluation and thus follow in the line of the traditional prudence of the Church.

When the first space capsule lifted off on its maiden voyage, the pilot was only thinking of the mission that had been entrusted to him from this point on. Back on the ground the designers and technicians were responsible for meticulously watching for any weakness or possible deviation in the functioning of the system. In the same way, the Church lives by functions and charisms that are complementary.

I should add here some further remarks based on my visits to Medjugorje in May and June of 1984 after I had composed the main body of the text of this book.

The first of these further visits took place at a time when the expanded Commission appointed by Bishop Žanić held its first meetings on March 23-24 of this year. Those who were chosen for the Commission were among the most critically-minded of the available experts and they were, for the most part, opposed to the authenticity of the apparitions. The Commission's final statement, widely published in the press, calls for a spirit of analysis and recommends that those who see the apparitions and those who are making them known maintain silence until there has been a judgment on the part of the Bishop, who has been instructed by the Holy See to avoid a hasty conclusion.

There was no doctor at the first meeting of this commission. It was a priest, Fr. Nicolas Bulat, professor of theology at Split, who pricked the young people with needles during an ecstasy. They were unaware of it. We can hope that doctors will soon be able to play a role in this commission. It is also desired that the Commission take into consideration the scientific tests already undertaken by Dr. Botta of Milan (electrocardiogram on March 24, 1984) and Dr. Joyeux of Montpellier (electroencephalogram on June 10, 1984). Dr. Joyeux's test shows that during the ecstasy the young people are neither dreaming nor in any kind of epileptic state. Finally, it is to be desired that those who undertake serious enquiry will not be excluded from the Commission by the fact that they are favorable to the apparitions.

There are two reasons for thinking that the apparitions will soon end. First, the duration of the apparitions has been constantly diminishing. They lasted about 20 minutes in the summer of 1983, about two minutes in December 1983 and have lasted about a minute from January 1984 until the time of this writing. The second reason is that the progressive revelation of the secrets has reached a point where all of them know nine of the secrets except Marjana who knows all ten and Vicka who knows eight. I said to Vicka "you are behind time." She said to me: "No, it is Our Lady who is behind time with me."

The prolonging of the apparitions to an apparently excessive degree is justified by the spiritual formation that the young people and those of the town are receiving to an ever-greater degree. This is a major aspect of Medjugorje.

At the end of May 1984, Helena and Mirjana, with whom I spoke on June 10, had received from the Virgin a call to celebrate August 5 as the 2,000th anniversary of her birth. The feast was to be celebrated by two days of fasting and a day of celebration. The Bishop ordered that the preaching at Medjugorje not mention this anniversary nor the feast of August 5, so that there would not be any competition with the feast of Mary's birth, celebrated by the Church on September 8. These orders were scrupulously followed. August 5 was celebrated very intensely but very discreetly. The three days of fast (they added one) ended in a day of intense prayer in the Church and on the hill. There were many conversions and confessions. One of the priests said to me: "I will remember this day more than my 20 previous years as a confessor." According to the young people, Mary had said that the priests who had heard confessions that day would have great joy.

Other aspects of Medjugorje, about which I have gained new information or insight, are included in their proper place in this edition of the book. We are watching an artist at work and his painting is not yet finished. We must be attentive to all that is still transpiring at Medjugorje if we wish to understand the total message. We must be ready to hear and obey what the Lord is saying to us through the message of Mary at Medjugorje, through our own daily contact with his Word in the Scriptures, and in the movement of the Holy Spirit who is guiding the Church.

Pronunciation Guide

The following is a key to help the reader pronounce the Croatian proper names in this book.

c	ts, as in *lots*
č and ć	ch, as in *change*
š	sh, as in *marsh*
ž	s, as in *pleasure*
j	y, as in *yes*
dj	j, as in *major*
i	ee, as in *feet*
e	e, as in *net*
u	oo, as in *soon*
a	a, as in *father*

The road to Medjugorje.

Chapter One

Are There Apparitions At Medjugorje?

A Sign Of Contradiction Or Good News?

> We know with absolute certainty that frequent miracles, innumerable benefits, spiritual visions, heavenly revelations and great consolations from the Mother of God abound until that time when the aged world will reach its end at the dawn of the kingdom which will never end.
>
> *(Amadeus of Lausanne, Homily 8)*

Good News?

EVER SINCE THE SUMMER OF 1981 PEOPLE HAVE BEEN TALKING about apparitions of the Virgin Mary at Medjugorje. Medjugorje is in Yugoslavia, in the Catholic Croatian region of Hercegovina. These apparitions began on June 24, 1981 and are still continuing. What does this mean; why should we be speaking about it? Is this the Good News of the Gospel, a sign of the times?

In recent years, in the free world of Western Europe, apparitions seem no longer to occur or at least they are not recognized or accepted. In the nineteenth century and in the early part of this century there have been a remarkable series of apparitions of the Virgin Mary. To mention only those apparitions which have been recognized, we have La Rue du Bac (1830), La Salette (September 19, 1846), Lourdes (1858), and Pontmain (January 17, 1871). These have continued in the 20th century, first at Fatima and then in Belgium at

Beauraing and Banneux (1933). But it seems that such things have come to an end. It is not that these latest apparitions have had the character of some final word. It is rather that no other apparitions have been recognized since. Fatima and Belgium took place over 50 years ago and even at that time they encountered serious difficulty in being recognized. The first bishop responsible for Beauraing, Bishop Heylen, was deprived of his normal authority and right to pass judgment.

May we conclude that there are no more apparitions in the life of the Church? The phenomenon has continued. Dom Bernard Billet has drawn up a list of over 200 presumed apparitions which have been reported since the 1930's, but none of them have been recognized. Should we consider that they are all illusions? Is it not rather that they took place in a cultural and ecclesial environment in which they could never have been recognized?

Whether they were authentic or not, doubt and denial prevailed in every case (whether it was good or bad). Real discernment such as that made by Bishop Laurence at Lourdes, in a manner exemplary for his day, does not seem possible any longer. Some commissions composed of people dominated by radical presuppositions [these presuppositions are derived from the historical-critical method or psychoanalysis, or people imbued with rationalistic or idealistic philosophies—outlooks which are found more often among our Catholic intelligentsia than at first appears] could never arrive at a positive judgment concerning these apparitions.

I have shocked people every once in a while in these recent years by saying that if Lourdes were to take place in our own day the apparitions would not be recognized. There would be enormous objections raised in the confused period which followed the apparitions. When the apparitions ceased on April 11, 1858 an epidemic of visionaries broke out; there were nearly 50 of them. The outbreak made a strong impression on the local pastor who had been so severe with Bernadette and won the enthusaism of Jean-Baptiste Estrade, an intelligent man and future historian of Lourdes. A few visionary types and questionable people, drawn by the prestige of the apparitions, showed up at the grotto of Lourdes. They seemed to pick up where Bernadette left off. In our own day Bernadette's exemplary witness would probably be reduced, by the use of a few catch words, to another instance of the same epidemic: this is a teenager, one whose adolescence has been retarded or in whom a combination of factors makes anything possible when it comes to visions, etc. A ready-made psychoanalytic grid would be applied in a superficial, confident way in order to explain the apparitions as a purely natural phenomenon that has nothing to do with God. I have seen this done. Given the prevalent deterministic atmosphere, God seems forbidden to perform any miracles at all.

This difficulty is aggravated by a deficient methodology governing the judgment concerning miracles. In principle it is required that the miracle in question be a prodigy completely inexplicable by science. This is not in keeping with God's way of acting or with the tradition of the Church. According to modern criteriology, the ideal miracle, that which our modern norms would allow, would be more magic than miracle. It would be a physical event taking place outside any realm of faith. Inner healings are excluded from these reports whenever they do not result from an organic healing. The typical miracle, however, is a divine action which goes from the interior to the exterior: a healing from sin which moves to an inner healing and finally a physical healing.

There is no need to put our hypercritical era on trial here. Its illusions may already be out of date. Rather, I wish to insist on the fact that attempts to make the necessary discernment have gone to unacceptable lengths. This is not the place to propose a new criteriology more in keeping with both modern science and theology; I have done that elsewhere. It is rather a question of pinpointing the roots of the hypercritical mentality in order to foster a better discernment.

Generally speaking, we can distinguish three different moments or historical periods in the Church. At the beginning the faith of the Christians rested on the appearances of the risen Christ. These are the foundation of the faith even though they do not have the nature of a scientific proof and were not to be forced on those who opposed them. A theology which would make light of the importance of these apparitions would be making a grave mistake.

After these foundational appearances, other appearances, rather frequently reported in the Acts of the Apostles, were of a secondary nature according to the norm described by Christ himself: "Blessed are those who have not seen and yet have believed" (Jn. 20:29).

The third period is that of faith which is based on the word of God without visible support, as the Letter to the Hebrews describes it. Now, apparitions have only a secondary role. They are of relative importance, and of exceptional occurrence. They are a gratuitous, provisional gift accorded by God to men and women on their pilgrimage. That is why the authority of the Church fosters a very great restraint in these matters and does not admit them without a very rigorous scrutiny.

In the course of centuries three factors contributed to augmenting this rigor.

1) The Montanist charismatic movement of the third century, a new surge of prophecy begun in such a promising way, became tainted with excesses that gave rise to tensions and, ultimately, to a schism. The Church still carries the effects of the trauma. Perplexed, the Church has recognized the admirable doctrine of Tertullian, who is counted among the Fathers of the Church, even though he belonged to the Montanist schism. Ultimately, the traumatic effects prevailed.

Since that time, ecclesiastical authority has often been very strict when faced with visions, charisms, and extraordinary phenomena. It is always a problem for officially established authority when "spiritual" people or visionaries arise whose direct line to God acquires an authority greater than their own. A bishop is all the more likely to fear a rise of such parallel authority to the degree that the communication with heaven which passes back and forth can be colored by the subjectivity of the visionary. Then, too, those in authority can tend to be hardened when their own degree of holiness leaves something to be desired.

This seems to have been the case with certain fervent religious groups in the Middle Ages who followed in the wake of the Franciscans. Francis of Assisi himself was well-accepted, despite some apprehension, because of his marvelous obedience and love. Other movements and small groups which emerged in his train were so completely repressed that we usually know nothing about them except through the caricatures of their opponents. As a result, it is often very difficult to distinguish between the heretics and fervent, upright groups who were somewhat troublesome and often calumniated. Happily, the papacy and the Church's episcopacy are no longer what they were in the time when repression went as far as having Savonarola, that fearsome denouncer of the abuses of the 15th century Church, burnt at the stake.

2) Another influence opposed to apparitions began when theology became the property of the university. Up to that point theology had been rather the domain of bishops, because of the teaching function conferred upon them at their ordination, or monks, because of their prayer and spiritual experience. At the university, effort was concentrated on abstraction, rational discourse, and intellectual performance. The height of science was the third degree of abstraction. In the wake of this Greek rationality, the new stage of theology tended to undervalue symbols and signs as the by-products of fanciful imag-

ination. Thus, there was a rupture between theological reason, which was sometimes cold-blooded, and signs, which are essential not only to popular religion but also to biblical revelation and to religion itself. The result was a certain lack of balance and excessive mistrust of signs from heaven.

3) Another wave of thought which tended to depreciate and reduce signs and symbols arose in the 19th century. It had its antecedents in the 18th century when the scientific spirit and a new cult of reason arose. The philosophers of the Enlightenment (18th century) popularized this current of thought. The kind of rationalism which adopted a reductionist stance in regard to symbols and the supernatural was sharpened during the 19th century by the ideals of German Criticism. The admirable concern for scientific rigor became systematic suspicion and reductionism. Methodological doubt became thoroughgoing. The negative aspects of criticism first ravaged the Protestant communities. This was the movement of liberal Protestantism which entered into post-Conciliar Catholicism in the 1960's just when the Protestants were turning away from it.

D. F. Strauss, professor of Hegelian philosophy and exegesis, gave expression to a rationalistic current of thought rendered more complex by the idealism of Kant and Hegel. According to this outlook, God cannot intervene in the order of this universe. Miracles and marvelous occurrences (biblical or other) must be held to be subjective illusions. Psychoanalysis gave another impetus to this ideology. According to Marc Oraison, a Catholic priest, any vision or apparition should be considered a "hallucination" and should be explained in terms of the psychological mechanisms of the subject. What is most striking in this outlook is the facility with which the investigators, using an *a priori* reductionism, explain every apparition or miracle in keeping with their system without an attentive examination of the facts or any verification of their own hypotheses.

Here is not the place to combat this artificial and often naive criticism: "The whistle sounds and disappears in the night." Still less is there any intention of rejecting all criticism. Criticism is a good and necessary undertaking. The word comes from the Greek *krisis*, (judgment) and signifies that discernment which is absolutely necessary in all things. If there is a need to critique the criticism when it systematically and *a priori* excludes the supernatural and any communication with God, this is because it thus blocks any discernment in the name of a systematic ideology. It is necessary, then, to evaluate, that is, to discern spiritual phenomena. This should be done with full knowledge of what is involved, not forgetting human complexity and the ambiguity of these exceptional spiritual occurrences. There is no easy formula which will enable us to disentangle the role played by the human psyche and subjectivity, which are necessarily involved in such experiences, and the role played by God.

The End of Hypercriticism

There is even less reason to concentrate on the abuses of much recent critical analysis because these rationalistic exaggerations have been by-passed by new stages in the growth of science itself. Science has begun to grasp the mysterious complexity of the world. That kind of science is dead which used to think it could say, "Miracles are impossible," "The soul does not exist, I have never found it in any surgical operation," and other similarly naive statements. The very fidelity to experience, so essential to scientific method, has shown that we cannot easily determine *a priori* what is reasonable and what is not. Science in the 20th century has made progress because it has been open to apparently irrational conclusions: relativity, the relation of uncertainty of Eisenberg, etc. Science, which has become more and more open to experience and more and more aware of its own limits (and of the impossibility of imposing laws on reality in the name of a simplistic rationalism), has become an example of humility in the face of reality.

This new openness of true science has not yet sufficiently penetrated into the domain of some theology called "critical." However, this openness has made an impression within the Church and in popular opinion; it has created an atmosphere more favorable for authentically discerning the gifts of God. One may wish to call such things "supernatural," a word which is itself ambiguous and relative, or one may prefer to use an image, as did Bishop Laurence at Lourdes in 1862: "The finger of God is here."

At San Damiano in Assisi, John Paul II (who has made many pilgrimages to places of apparitions—Guadalupe, Lourdes, Fatima—) tactfully proposed substituting an enlightened control of data in place of a systematic denial. Without a doubt a lot of wasted energy could have been saved if this principle had prevailed in pastoral practice.

The new event at Medjugorje is still too surrounded by a situation of conflict for us to be able to see clearly. It will take some years of peace. However, these events can be full of promise if those involved know how to welcome them moderately and in a spirit of obedience to the Church.

A Sign of the Times

Medjugorje is very different and very new; it has an atmosphere which in many ways is characteristic of the post-Conciliar era. The six recipients of the apparition are no longer children (with one possible exception). They are 16 to 18 years old; they have gone beyond the years of adolescence. These apparitions have profoundly changed their lives as well as that of the parish and the entire region. All this has taken place in a nation where atheistic Marxism governs life with a power well-known. That these signs from heaven would take place in an atheistic environment, one that has been so well controlled for a half century, is already a sign of the times. This is said without anticipating a judgment in favor of the apparitions concerning which the Church has made no pronouncement. I say it based on a vision of the whole situation: these apparitions are not an isolated phenomenon. They are part of a complex of spiritual events taking place in a country where the faith is strangled, repressed, asphyxiated. They are taking place at a time when the faith in the countries of the West is becoming somnolent or is disintegrating. At a time when Christian historians are making light of the heroism of the early Church's martyrs, we see a new heroism arising in the face of a persecution which is less bloody but much more far-reaching and pervasive. It includes the manipulation of the human psyche in an attempt to destroy those consigned to psychiatric hospitals on the principle that faith is a psychological illness. The gifts of grace which hold these countries erect have given rise to a renewal of faith which is irrepressible in Poland, and less known but no less real in other countries. This new reality has shifted the Church's center of gravity, moving it to those places of courage and fidelity. The election of a Polish pope is but one more sign among others.

Supernatural occurrences in the countries of the East are not usually known except through personal testimony, and they cannot be widely communicated without danger of fierce repression of those who are living these gifts of God in an heroic way. Because I have a personal knowledge of many of these examples of God's action, I gave a positive welcome to the events of Medjugorje as being possibly another instance of the Good News.

These events were able to make themselves known in a country which lies on the border between East and West—Yugoslavia: a Marxist country, but more independent than the others. For a long time Yugoslavia has maintained a particular set of relationships with the West. Even during Tito's lifetime, it established diplomatic relations with the Catholic Church and accepted a papal nunciature. In this country the inexorable rigor of Marxism is tempered by the existence of a people careful to guard their independence. It has elicited the respect of both West and East because of its courage in maintaining a certain autonomy, in organizing its alliances in an original manner, in allowing more freedom than elsewhere for emigration, and in being open to welcome visitors from the outside.

Yugoslavia is not Albania. An event of religious nature could appear there much more easily than in those countries which insure a much more complete repression of religion. It is simple justice to point out this favorable aspect of Yugoslavia, one which is full of hope and which allows a certain latitude to Christianity. Yugoslavia is a Mediterranean land, and therefore human. This serves to temper many systems.

However, that does not mean that we should think of the condition of the Christians as being happy or even easy. The Church in Croatia, which heroically survived Muslim domination for many centuries, is now subjected to a harsh system of laws. Its people suffer from the atheistic regime more than others in the Yugoslavian federation. Thus the sign from heaven seems to be quite providential in this Church on the point of asphyxiation.

What Does the Church Think?

What does the Church in Yugoslavia think of all of this? More precisely, what does the local bishop think?

The bishop responsible in this matter is Bishop Pavao Žanić. His attitude is one of discernment and prudence in keeping with the true tradition of the Church. He neither uses the apparitions as a means of waging war against the government nor does he battle against those who are experiencing these extraordinary events. He is waiting and observing; he really cannot do otherwise since the apparitions are still going on. They are a symphony as yet incomplete, and the last notes will be of supreme importance in discernment. And then again, a supernatural reality, even when it is authentic, can always contain a certain admixture of elements which are less authentic.

Lourdes did not escape this danger, as we have seen. Even something authentic can go astray given the weakness and sin which are never absent from our world. The authority of the Church must always be alert against the assaults of the tempter, which will never be lacking. Actually, the Bishop's concern is less to recognize various hypotheses than to foresee them, including negative hypotheses: this can seem disappointing to an excessive hopefulness.

We must be very clear here. At this actual stage of events, there is no room for triumphalism. The authority of the Church has not passed judgment. Rather, it is following the events and encouraging discernment among those who are living through them. This includes the recipients of the apparitions, the priests, the faithful in prayer, and those who feel themselves to be involved in any way, including theologians like myself. Along with Father Rupčić and in continuity with his efforts, I wish only to bring to these events the clarifying aid of a knowledge of history and theology which is the fruit of some 30 years of study. I wish to maintain a twofold respect—for those who are living through this unusual adventure, and for the episcopal authority which carries the heavy responsibility for it.

I say heavy responsibility because Yugoslavia, though it is a modern and open country, is still officially atheistic. It promotes, deliberately and officially, the cause of atheism with all the dialectic and administrative power of a modern state in which the police and the other administrative resources have assumed an importance unknown to previous centuries.

If the Bishop of Mostar had imprudently declared himself in favor of the apparitions, too quickly and without any qualifications, he could have brought about a series of reprisals. The unusual prolongation of the apparitions also invites one to be particularly prudent. However, his has not been an inactive or passive prudence. When the government tried to ridicule the apparitions, making a caricature of them in order to facilitate their repression, the Bishop intervened. Near the middle of August of 1981, this courageous declaration appeared in *Glas Koncila* (*The Voice of the Council*, Zagreb, August 16, 1981, p. 1):

1. The public is waiting for us to say something about the events at Medjugorje, where the children assert that the Virgin has appeared to them and continues to appear to them. When those who report on these events are atheistic journalists who believe neither in God nor in the Virgin, it is normal that they should deny any truth in what the children are saying. For us, however, the believers, this way of treating the events is offensive and unacceptable. Without any proof they are accusing the children of being manipulated.

2. The articles which are appearing in the press are written by people who, starting out from a position of power, approach

questions of faith and religion with irony and suspicion and make accusations without any proof. Among the numerous insinuations, they accuse the priests of "gathering these small children and teaching them, without the knowledge of their parents, to pretend that the Virgin has appeared to them in human form."

3. It is equally false to say that the ecclesiastical authorities have taken up a stand against the events at Bijakovići, declaring them to be superstitious. We also regret that the Church of Hercegovina is accused of mixing in politics and desiring to fool the public.

4. Concerning apparitions and miracles in general, we must say that, for us believers, they are possible. We cannot deny Jesus Christ or the lives of the Saints. On the other hand, it is well known that the Church has always been very prudent before offering a positive judgment concerning the apparitions and miracles at Lourdes, Fatima and elsewhere.

5. It is true that pious people have often asserted that they saw apparitions when these were rather hallucinations, personal psychological experiences, or pure imagination.

6. What are we able to say about what is happening at Bijakovići? One thing is certain, the children are not being urged by anyone, least of all by the Church, to be making untruthful declarations. For the moment, everything leads us to the conviction that the children are not lying. The more difficult question remains: are we dealing with a purely subjective experience on the part of the children or with a supernatural event?

7. We read in the Acts of the Apostles that, when the Jews tried to silence the apostles, a teacher of the law, one highly esteemed by all the people, Gamaliel, said to the whole assembly: "If their purpose or activity is of human origin, it will fail. But, if it is from God, you will not be able to stop it" (Acts 5:38-39).

This is the position that we adopt for the moment.

Pavao Žanić, Bishop of Mostar

When the attacks of the public authorities were renewed, the Bishop of Mostar, on September 1, 1981, sent a letter to the president of the Federal Republic of Yugoslavia, Sergej Krajger, in which he lodged the following protest:

Mr. President,
In the newspapers, on the radio and the television, the news was given us that on August 17, 1981, there took place at Čitluk a meeting of the communal conference of the Socialist Union of the Working People of Čitluk. At this meeting the events taking place

in the parish of Medjugorje were discussed and the following text was released to the news.

"It was decided that it is necessary to explain again to the people more clearly that what the priests Jozo Zovko of Medjugorje and his colleague Ferdo Vlašić, Pavao Žanić, the Bishop of Mostar, and other extremists intend and desire is nothing other than to bring about the dream and project of the terroristic Ustaša organization. All of this constitutes the gravest abuse of religious sentiment." (Taken from the radio-television news of Sarajevo, August 17, 1981, and from the newspaper, *Večernji List*, August 18, 1981).

I consider it my duty and my right to protest forcefully against such calumnies totally devoid of any foundation. As the Catholic Bishop and the Ordinary responsible for the Diocese of Mostar, for my own part and for that of my priests who have been implicated, I am saddened by these irresponsible calumnies and these attacks whose bad taste will in no way help to assess serenely the events which have taken place in the parish of Medjugorje.

By such proceedings the fundamental rights of a man and a citizen are violated.

I ask you to accept my protestation—which I address to the person who holds the highest responsibility in Yugoslavia—and I ask you to react firmly against such attacks.

I ask you to accept this expression of my respect.

Pavao Žanić, Bishop of Mostar

On January 10, 1982, the Bishop established a committee of inquiry to look into the apparitions. We will see further how the Bishop was led to attribute a certain value to various objections against Medjugorje and to set himself in opposition to the growing conviction in favor of the apparitions which seemed to him to be excessive, even irresponsible propaganda. He came to the point of asking himself the question: "How is it possible to take precautions against what could be a serious and ruinous deception if one day this spiritual phenomenon proves to be illusory?" This reticence, which we will situate and examine further on when we evaluate, does not constitute in any way a negative judgment on the part of the Bishop. After having defended Medjugorje against calumnies, he considers it a duty as well to defend it against the risks of an excessive or premature confidence. His position remains deliberately that of waiting and seeing, according to the principle of Gamaliel, which he recalled so well: "If their purpose or activity is of human origin, it will fail. But, if it is from God, you will not be able to stop it" (Acts 5:38-39).

What You Will Find in This Book

The basis of this book is constituted by the translation from Croatian of the book by Father Rupčić, *The Apparitions of the Virgin at Medju gorje*, Samobor, A. G. Matoš, 1983 (176 pp.). Father Rupčić is an exegete, a man used to critical reflection. He methodically questioned those who received the visions. He had the courage to be the first to publish a history and an evaluation of the apparitions. It is a contribution which is new, original, and serious. His book, however, was but a first step. It was never intended to be a complete or fully developed history.

It is not complete because the book was finished in 1982. The author restricted himself to the first seven apparitions and merely gave a general overview of the rest. He did not give a report on any of the further apparitions which now number nearly a thousand.

To compose a fully developed history of the apparitions would be a gigantic task. Perhaps it will never be possible. Too many factors are involved which prevent the gathering of all the desirable documentation. There are, certainly, photographs, films, tape recordings, and a large quantity of notes. But there is room to think that all these are deficient in varying degrees in regard to a good number of the apparitions. The first chronicle of the parish was confiscated by the police, and the fear of what a hostile authority could make of further documentation dissuaded people from writing.

The prudence demanded in an atheistic country often obliged Father Rupčić to be discreet, even vague. He had first-hand information which, however, had no pretensions of being complete, and Father Rupčić himself did not wish to divulge all that he knew. He avoided giving the names of the witnesses whom he cited, and he restricted himself to a general summary of the message without citing the words of Mary. This procedure demands, for a Western public, a certain amount of adaptation and addition. Certain details are now available, and we have not hesitated to add them whenever it was possible. The author himself has encouraged us to do this, and we were able on December 24-26, 1983 to submit the first adaptation to him. When we were with him, we were able to gather new information worthy of interest.

A book written in the East can never fully accord with the expectations of a Western audience. Questions and points of reference are not the same. The Christians in the Church of silence write with many allusions, innuendos, and vague references which have become second nature. We can only admire the amazing performance of

Father Rupčić in Yugoslavia. His art of being able to sort out and tone down his narrative enabled him to publish the book within the country itself. The style, however, requires some adaptation for a Western public. This work of adaptation is solely my responsibility. I thank the author and others (whom I also am not always able to cite) for the information given me, for their confidence and their understanding. I am aware of the risks in such an undertaking. I did not do it without the fear of losing certain values of the original text, even if it was for the benefit of the Western reader who would not have been able to appreciate or accept the book without this work of adaptation.

The apologetic aspect of this book also required adaptation for a Western audience. Our critical spirit (sometimes hypercritical) requires arguments that are more concrete, a presentation of data which is more precise, and greater reserve regarding conclusions so that these do not seem to be unwarranted by the data. Therefore, we have tried to strengthen the arguments and to modify the conclusions.

Such adaptation is impossible without direct knowledge of the events. For that reason it soon became apparent to me that I would have to go to Medjugorje myself. Therefore, on December 23, 1983, I took the plane to Yugoslavia in order to spend Christmas at Medjugorje and to meet those who are responsible for discerning.

Surprises at Medjugorje

From the moment I arrived in Yugoslavia, I became aware of the difficulties which are always present in that country. When I disembarked at the airport at 9:00 in the evening (the plane was two hours late), my visit began with an interrogation and a searching of my luggage which took two hours. I was allowed to accept the delivery of the car I had rented. This was a sign of good will because the rental agency was waiting for me before closing. My interrogation followed that of Father Rupčić. It took place in the police station of the airport and was conducted by a man who was both intelligent and courteous. He seemed to fear that I came as a political emissary from some Yugoslavians who had previously emigrated.

I responded to him with the same courtesy: "Because there is no basis for this interrogation, it's a shame that a man of your status and importance has to waste his time and to cause me to waste mine as well. If you really have any doubts in my regard, you can search my briefcase and my luggage, and you will find nothing suspect. But even then it is a shame because, after all that, you will have to beg pardon of me." He answered me: "If I have made a mistake, I ask your pardon in advance."

There then followed a very careful investigation. Sheet by sheet he looked at all my files which, happily, I had lightened before leaving. He had his clerk note all the proper names, particularly those of the sick who had been healed at Medjugorje (I had gotten these from the book of Father Rupčić, already well-known in Yugoslavia). He then went on to look at, one after the other, all the items in my press file, which I had brought along with me, as I always do. I told him that, out of courtesy, I had taken out some articles which were critical, as there always are in the press, and that he would find nothing there but the newspapers that are on sale on the newsstands of Yugoslavia. He carried the investigation to its conclusion. However, he omitted examining my voluminous notebook of addresses, in which there were no Yugoslav names. The investigation ended with no result.

The official surpassed himself in courtesy. He himself carried my heavy suitcase to the car along a route which measured about 500 yards. I would have wished to lighten his task by pointing out to him that the suitcase had wheels on it which would have made the job much easier. However, the interpreter wasn't there and the prudence of my companion opted for this honorable solution to the problem without risking any more words.

Yugoslavia is a country which welcomes tourists. Were they afraid that Medjugorje might become a tool for propaganda? That is possible. But the police were torn between this unfounded fear and the desire not to tarnish their image as a hospitable land. The examination ended there, though it was followed by a very discreet surveillance.

Another Book about Medjugorje

There was another surprise. Just when I began to revise the partial translation of the book of Father Rupčić, which had been carefully and competently done by Vera Knežević, I received a phone call from the charismatic community, Lion of Judah: "It seems that you are getting ready to publish the translation of a book on the apparitions of Medjugorje. We are also preparing to publish that translation with the Fayard Publishing Company."

Because I have no competence in this sort of legal problem, I suggested that the editors discuss the matter among themselves.   19

When everything was considered, it was not the same book at all which we were getting ready to publish. Besides that, it can only be an advantage for the public at large to have two complementary accounts concerning a subject which is so complex. Therefore, my preoccupation was not to harmonize the two books but rather to maintain their differences, except that I omitted this or that item of documentation which is found published in the other book.

The book translated by the Lion of Judah community in France is that of Svetozar Kraljević, a Franciscan. It has been edited in English by Father Michael Scanlan, president of Steubenville University, and published by the Franciscan Herald Press under the title of *The Apparitions of Mary at Medjugorje*. I met Fr. Kraljević in Yugoslavia. He is a cultured man, sensitive, charismatic, and open to changing his opinion. He used to teach in the United States, but his passport was rescinded, as also happened to Father Rupčić. Their commitment to Medjugorje seems to have been the problem.

Father Kraljević's book was adapted in French by Ephraim Croissant of the Lion of Judah community. Added to this is the testimony of Dr. Philippe Madre of the same community. Dr. Madre, along with Fr. Émiliano Tardif, of the Missionaries of the Sacred Heart, and Fr. Pierre Rancourt visited Medjugorje from Tuesday, August 23, 1983, until Thursday, August 25. They were there in order to bring to the spontaneous presence of charisms at Medjugorje the experience of the charismatic renewal, particularly in regard to the gift of healing. There had been many healings at Medjugorje and many people asking for healings. It was important to benefit from a correct convergence of the two spiritual currents.

This visit was in keeping with bonds that had been established for quite some time. In May 1981, before the apparitions, Fr. Tomislav Vlašić, a Franciscan from Hercegovina, participated in a meeting for leaders in the charismatic renewal held in Rome. At that time there were two prophecies in his regard: Sr. Briege McKenna, in prophecy saw him seated in the midst of a great crowd and from where he was seated there flowed rivers of living water. Fr. Émiliano Tardif felt led to pronounce a prophecy in the name of the Lord which said, "Do not fear. I am sending you my Mother."

At that time Fr. Vlašić was not at Medjugorje. The apparitions took place at a time when another group of Franciscans was responsible for the parish. When the pastor, Fr. Jozo Zovko, was put in prison because of the apparitions and his assistant, who then became responsible, preferred to go elsewhere, Fr. Tomislav was appointed to Medjugorje. He became co-pastor along with Fr. Tomislav Pervan.

Thus began in a more concrete way the harmony already established between the apparitions and the charismatic renewal.

The three visitors, Dr. Madre, and Frs. Tardif and Rancourt (both originally from Quebec) arrived at 6:00 on Tuesday, August 23. Their time there was fruitful but brief—hardly a day and a half. On Thursday, at 1:30 p.m. the ever-watchful police arrested the three preachers, interrogated them, searched them, put them in prison, and freed them the next day at 1:30 p.m., giving them the choice between leaving the country before midnight or returning to prison. This was accompanied by a prohibition against visiting for a year.

Philippe Madre gives the report of an observer who is at the same time a committed participant familiar with the spiritual adventure of Medjugorje from the inside. His is the expression of a witness (*martyrion* in Greek) aware of having a mission to make the message known and of having evidence.

This book attempts to discern Medjugorje according to the principles already applied in my previous studies of La Rue du Bac, Lourdes, Pontmain and in my book, *Miracles in El Paso?*

Father Rupčić's book published in Yugoslavia contains a long treatment of the problem of apparitions in general. These questions have already been studied at great length in western Europe. In French, after having published various monographs, I devoted a book to this question: it is entitled *Les Routes De Dieu* and is published by O.E.I.L. in the series "Sanctuaries, Pilgrimages, Apparitions." There is no reason, therefore, to repeat this theoretical basis for the study which follows, as Fr. Rupčić did so usefully for his Yugoslav audience. Here, rather, it is a question of applying those principles to discerning the events at Medjugorje, which are still fresh and new, and where, for the first time in my life, I personally saw ecstasy.

Enough of explanations. Here is the study by Fr. Rupčić, published with his help. It has the nature of a first report, coming before a more fully developed history. This will be written when the apparitions are over and the promises (still secret) which were confided to the young people are fulfilled in a way which no one can predetermine now. The young people know what the sign promised at the end of the apparitions will be, and when it will happen; but they are still obliged to keep this to themselves. It remains, historically and theologically, an unknown reality.

An account of the first apparitions (by Fr. Rupčić) and further developments will be followed by our evaluation.

René Laurentin

The six youngsters. From left to right:
Vicka, Jakov, Mirjana, Ivanka, Marija,
and Ivan.

Crosses placed at the location of the
first apparition on the hill of Podbro.

The parish of Medjugorje is dominated
by the cross erected in 1933 on Sipovac
Hill. This cross (Kriz) resulted in the
name of the mountain being changed to
Križevać.

Chapter Two

The First
Seven Apparitions
On The Hill

The Double Apparition of Wednesday, June 24, 1981

THE APPARITIONS BEGAN ON WEDNESDAY, JUNE 24, 1981, THE feast of St. John the Baptist. On that day two young girls, Ivanka Ivanković and Mirjana Dragicević, whose families lived in the village of Bijakovići in the parish of Medjugorje, went out to take a walk on the mountain. Suddenly, Ivanka saw ahead of her a luminous silhouette. It was an indistinct form of a young girl in a gray robe, whose face was shining gently. She was hovering about a yard off the ground.

Ivanka murmured as though she spoke to herself, "Look, it's the Virgin Mary!" Mirjana shrugged her shoulders, "No, it couldn't be the Virgin Mary."

The two of them were afraid. They left the place and told others what they had seen. They left a message for Vicka Ivanković, who was taking a nap, tired from school: "When you wake up, come over to Jakov's house."

On the way Vicka found Ivan Ivanković (the oldest of the group, 20 years old) and Ivan Dragicević, 16, who were picking apples. They went along. Milka Pavlović, 13, went along with them.

Just as the first time, Ivanka saw something first: "There she is!" Mirjana was with her. The six young people were so overwhelmed that they did not dare say anything to the apparition. Afraid, they went back down the mountain to their homes and told people what they had seen. Nobody believed them.

Some people made fun of them. Marija, Milka's sister (who was to see for herself the next day), laughed at this new figment of her imagination. Vicka's sister told her: "You saw a flying saucer."

Nevertheless, the village was talking about the event well into the night. With regard to the young people, they couldn't sleep. They waited for the next day with impatience.

The Second Apparition, Thursday, June 25

The next day, June 25, at the same time (6:15 p.m.) the six young people, along with two older persons whom they took as witnesses, returned to the place of the apparition. It is a rise on the side of the hill, which is called *Podbrdo* ("foot of the hill"). As they were going, several among them caught a glimpse of the apparition for a moment. They were filled with joy. An impulse seized them, and they went up the hill on the run, "as though they had wings," without giving a thought to the hard, sharp stones or the brambles. Vicka was barefoot. In five minutes they were at the top, a trip which usually takes a good 20 minutes. The apparition was waiting for them there. An interior force made them kneel down. They began to pray. They were the only ones who saw anything; the two adults saw nothing.

Two of the young people from the first day had not come back. Ivan Ivanković, for whom the adventure of the day before seemed childish, and Milka Pavlović, sister of Marija and Filip Pavlović, who had to stay home because of work. "You have to stay here," her mother had told her. "Marija (the older girl, 15) can go." Marija, despite her skepticism of the previous evening, went.

Little Jakov Čolo, 10 years old, joined himself to the group, which was thus constituted once for all.

The four young people from the first day are:

1) Ivanka Ivanković, born April 21, 1966;

2) Vicka Ivanković, born July 3, 1964;

3) Mirjana Dragicević, born March 18, 1965;

4) Ivan Dragicević, born May 25, 1965 (no relation to Mirjana).

The two new young people, who came for the first time on June 25 are:

5) Marija Pavlović, born April 1, 1965;

6) Jakov Čolo, born June 3, 1971.

For the first time the young people spoke very simply with the apparition: "Why did she come?" Because she found faith here. She wished to ask for reconciliation and peace among everyone. They left the place brimming with happiness. From that time on it is to these six that the Virgin appears every day, except that Mirjana Dragicević stopped seeing the apparition after December 25, 1982. Since then the group has numbered five.

The Third Apparition, Friday, June 26

On the third day, June 26, at the time which had become usual (about 6:15 p.m.), a light appeared three times on the horizon in the direction of the place of the apparitions. The children ran up the hill at this signal. This time they went a little bit higher up (about 250 yards), rather far from one another, but all of a sudden something brought them together facing the northeast. They all knelt down at the same time.

The light which had brought them had been noticed. People came from all the villages of the area: Bijakovići, Medjugorje, Miletina, and as far away as Čitluk, the principal town of the area situated about five miles away.

So the crowd the third day was large; they say about two or three thousand. This human sea literally crushed them; Mirjana and Ivanka fainted. Marinko Ivanković, a neighbor who from then on became their protector, led them and a few others out of the crowd so that they could breathe.

Only the six young people saw the apparition. Milka, the sister of Marija, who had seen it the first day, came back this third day, but she did not see the apparition, and she has never seen it since. Why? She does not know. But she has never forgotten . . .

At first overwhelmed, the young people got bolder. They sang canticles; they asked the Virgin if she would come back the next day. She said nothing, but, with a movement of her head, she confirmed her return.

On that day the young people began to recite the Rosary, and the crowd joined in. They also recited for the first time a traditional prayer of the area: seven times the Our Father, Hail Mary, and Glory Be to the Father, to which the Virgin had them add the Creed.

Vicka, the most vivacious of the group, came with a bottle of holy water. She sprinkled the apparition saying: "If you are really Our Lady, then stay with us. If not, leave us." For an answer, the Virgin smiled.

Ivanka asked the Virgin about her mother, who had died two months earlier. It was to this orphan that Mary had first shown herself. In answer to this question, Our Lady responded that Ivanka should not worry. Her mother was happy near her. This was good news because Ivanka's mother did not have the reputation of being a "saint"; she was an ordinary mother of a family. Thus, as we understand it, Mary bore witness that the humble accomplishing of our human and Christian duties is a door to heaven.

The children asked the apparition: "Who are you?" She answered without ambiguity: "I am the Blessed Virgin Mary." The word "blessed" might seem surprising on Mary's lips, but this traditional expression used in her regard has nothing of triumphalism in it. It only signifies her perfect bliss.

After their question concerning her return and her sign of acquiescence, the children went back to their village peacefully. On that day the Virgin began to pronounce the key word of her message, which would be repeated in the apparitions to follow: "Peace! Peace! Peace! Be reconciled!" Her last words to them confirmed the message: "Go now in peace."

All of this is a striking anticipation of the theme upon which two years later, in 1983, both the Holy Year and the Synod of Bishops were to be centered.

Most of the crowd which had been present for the apparition went down the hill with the young people about 7:00 or 7:30 p.m. People helped Mirjana and Vicka down the hill. The heat was terrible; everyone was thirsty. They asked only for water, but the villagers went out of their way to offer the people all they had in the house to drink.

The Fourth Apparition, Saturday, June 27

On the morning of the fourth day, Saturday, June 27, the police began to be interested in the young people. They called them to Čitluk, the chief city of the area, for an interrogation. They questioned them at length and harshly, but the youngsters answered with a firmness that remained unshaken despite all dissuasions. They were then submitted to a psychiatric examination by Dr. Ante Vujević in a small ambulance, but the doctor declared them normal, balanced, and in good health.

When they got back home about noon, they had lunch and set out for Podbrdo. About 6:30 p.m. they were at the place of the apparitions, as on the preceding day: Vicka, Mirjana, Ivanka, Marija, Ivan Dragicević, and Jakov Čolo. These are the ones who have been present at all the subsequent apparitions.

The Fifth Apparition, Sunday, June 28

On the fifth day the weather was sunny and beautiful. The crowd which had come from the area all around was estimated to be about 15,000 people. The children came to their usual place; they knelt down. The Virgin was there! The crowd pressed around them; everyone wanted to be as close as possible to her. Despite the crush of the crowd, everything took place calmly.

Something new happened which was reported by one of the young people. At a certain moment the Virgin became sad. Someone in the crowd had blasphemed.

After the apparition the young people and the massive crowd went back down to the village. Again, everyone was thirsty. The villagers could have sold hundreds of gallons of drinks, but this never occurred to anyone. Everyone in the village brought out whatever he had in the house and offered it without charge. It was a festive day for the village.

The Sixth Apparition, Monday, June 29

On the sixth day, Monday, the police once again brought the young people to Čitluk for additional interrogation. The intention was to obtain a declaration concerning their psychological state with a view to committing them to a psychiatric ward. But these new medical examinations performed in the city of Mostar by Dr. Dzuda confirmed their perfect psychological balance.

The youngsters returned home and that same day, at the usual hour, they left for the meeting with Our Lady. They saw her, all six of them, as on the previous days. The crowd was even larger. However, the calm and good order remained untroubled. The young people prayed and sang, and the crowd joined in.

In their conversation with Mary, the children received this message addressed to everybody: "There is but one God, one faith, believe strongly, have confidence."

They asked the Virgin to heal little Danijel, who was mute and paralyzed. His parents were quite sad about his condition. "Let them believe firmly, and he will be healed," she said. This was to happen. Mary concluded: "Go in the peace of God." She disappeared. The light remained for an instant after her. She promised to return.

After the apparition, the villagers once more offered things to drink as on the previous day, though their resources were stretched once again by the size of the crowd.

The Seventh Apparition, At Cerno, Tuesday, June 30

On the next day, June 30, there was no apparition at Podbrdo—why not?

Two women, Ljubica Vasilj and Mirjana Ivanković, came to take the youngsters on a trip. The young people did not realize that the purpose was to get them far from the village and that the women had been asked to do this for just that purpose. Five of them got in the car provided for this happy excursion. Ivan Dragicević was not there.

It was a rather long trip: Čitluk (where the interrogations of the previous days had taken place), Žitomislić, Počitelje, the falls at Kravica, Ljubuški, etc.

Late in the afternoon, when the good women were sure that the time of the apparition had passed, they started home. However, a few miles from Bijakovići, the youngsters had a sense that they should ask the car to stop. The women at first refused but finally gave in, not having much doubt about what would happen.

They were by that time at Cerno near Ljubuški, in sight of the hill where the apparitions were taking place. From that height it is easy to see the Cross on the top of a hill about two miles away. The young people went aside to the right of the road which leads to Medjugorje. It was the time for their daily meeting with the Virgin. They knelt down. She was there.

They sang and prayed in her presence, as usual. The women heard the songs but did not understand very well.

Mirjana asked: "Were you annoyed that we weren't on the hill?" She answered: "It's nothing."

"Will you be annoyed if we don't go back to the hill but rather wait for you in the church?" Mirjana asked this question because the police had forbidden people to go to the usual place of the apparitions. The Virgin seemed to hesitate, then she agreed and concluded: "Go in the peace of God." She disappeared in the light.

Now the question was whether people should be told that the apparition would no longer take place on the hill. The youngsters discussed this with the pastor, Fr. Jozo Zovko. They would have preferred to be alone. However, it would be annoying to disappoint people and appear to be making fun of them. They knew that Our Lady came for the crowd as well. She had said: "Reconcile them."

After that the apparitions took place discreetly in the home of a neighbor who had a large room, then in the various homes of the young people. However, it was arranged to have Mass celebrated in the church after the time of the apparitions. The church is the one place where worship is authorized in the Marxist regime. It is there that the apparitions have taken place since January, 1982.

Up until the present (September, 1984) there have only been five days when the young people did not see the Virgin. These unexpected absences tend to confirm the fact that this is no make-believe on the part of the young people but rather something which takes place independently of their will. They really wanted to see the Virgin on the days that she did not come, and they were sad that they did not see her.

Most of the apparitions take place in the same way, though the youngsters do not know in advance if Our Lady will come or not. It is a pure and gratuitous grace. It is with a desire of seeing her that they pray every day. After the Rosary, in which they are joined by the large crowd which fills and overflows the church, they go aside. It is about 6:00 p.m. They go to a room just opposite the sacristy, near the altar. It is not even a chapel.

Some people are allowed to go with them into this special place; usually those who have asked some question or recommended a particular intention.

The room of the apparitions is small, about 14 by 15 feet. When they come into the room, the youngsters turn toward the Cross, which is on the northern wall. Then they put on a table just below the Cross objects which people have given to them—rosaries, pictures, etc.—so that Our Lady can bless them. They line up, facing the Cross, standing, and begin to recite seven times the Our Father, Hail Mary, and Glory Be to the Father, along with the Creed. This is the prayer that the Virgin recommended to them. Usually after the second or third Our Father, Our Lady appears to them in a great light which precedes her. At that moment the youngsters fall to their knees all at the same time in an impressive unison. Their gazes all converge in the same direction. Immobile and without any communication with the exterior world, they begin their dialogue with the Virgin. Those who are near them neither see nor hear anything. They are able only to observe the change that overtakes the young people: their gaze remains immobile, their faces are transfigured by an ecstatic happiness which is calm and moderate. Every once in a while their lips can be seen to move. They are involved in a conversation which cannot be heard. After a few minutes, their voices take up the prayer. They continue the Our Father (the first part is not heard): ". . . who art in heaven." They explain: "Our Lady starts it, and we take it up." They do this in perfect unison.

"The Virgin does not recite the Hail Mary," they add, "but we recite the Glory Be to the Father and the Creed with her." Sometimes they add the aspirations: "Behold the Cross! Behold the Heart!"

After a new period of silence during which the youngsters' lips continue to move, they enter into dialogue with the Virgin. After another period of silence, they stand up and begin to call to mind the answers the Virgin gave to the questions they transmitted to her. Then one or several of them will exclaim: "She is gone!" The apparition is over.

After the apparition, Mass is celebrated in the crowded church. The young people assist at Mass. They are not in the limelight, in fact, they are not even seen. Some sing in the choir, and some serve at the altar. At the end, everyone sings a hymn to the Virgin especially composed by Fr. Stanislas Vasilj. Before leaving the church, the youngsters recite seven times the Our Father, Hail Mary, and Glory Be to the Father, along with the Creed. The crowd joins them.

Such is the daily celebration of Mass in the parish church. The number assisting is quite large: never less than 1,000 people, sometimes as many as 10,000. As they are leaving, the young people pray for the sick, who ask for their prayers; sometimes there are many sick people. This can take about a half hour or a little longer.

It is only after all this that the young people return to their homes to do their chores or to take a rest. The next day, their day will be the same as that of all their classmates. They carry out all their duties, both in school and in the home, without asking for any special favors. They are just like all the other students. Were anyone to see them for the first time, they would not notice anything special, even if they looked closely, except that they are joyful, well moderated, generous at work, and obedient. Yes, perhaps that is what is "special" about the young people.

What The Young People See And Their Behavior

The young people state that they see Our Lady, "not a picture," but with three dimensions. "She is very beautiful" they say as best they can. They have difficulty finding suitable words to describe her. The colors and disposition of her clothes and her face go beyond any ordinary experience. They have never seen, "a young woman like her."

"She has black hair, a bit curly, blue eyes, rosy cheeks, she is slender . . . beautiful . . . light. I want to look at her, to look only at her . . . how beautiful she is. She is covered with a veil which flows over a robe which is impossible to describe."

"What color is the robe?"

"You could say it was gray, and yet it isn't quite gray. It's something like coffee with cream in it, but it isn't really that, either. I don't know any color like it." It is a luminous transparency akin to blue.

"Her voice is agreeable to listen to. You could say it was music. You could say she sings. She speaks Croatian."

Sometimes the youngsters have seen Jesus with her, his Heart, and the Cross. Some among them have also seen hell, heaven, and purgatory. Mirjana said that she saw the devil fleeing before the light which precedes the apparitions of the Virgin.

Those who see the apparition are amazed that those who are near them neither see nor hear anything. They perceive the Virgin as a very real person occupying three spatial dimensions. They seem to themselves to be seeing and touching her.

During the apparition they all have the same behavior and the same reactions, along with variations which correspond to what is said to them personally. This causes one to think that their behavior is not the manifestation of some unconscious desire, but rather the response to something exterior to them. This seems to exclude auto-suggestion or hallucination. The psychiatrists and psychologists who have examined them tend to confirm this judgment. (See especially: Slavko Barbarić: *Psycho-pedagogic Examination of the Visionaries of Medjugorje*, in the parish file, 1982, pp. 14, 17-19.)

Words and Messages

The apparition of the Virgin is itself a message. However, at the same time she conveys explicit statements: the world has an urgent need of faith, of prayer, of repentance, and of asceticism. It can be saved.

This message concerns the whole world, and those who experience the apparitions have the mission of spreading it. There are other messages which concern the young people themselves, others still which pertain to particular persons or groups who address a question to Our Lady. These messages are answers. Everything breathes an atmosphere of dignity, of seriousness, of wisdom and supernatural tact. Obviously, all of this far exceeds the intellectual capacities of the six, who are but ordinary young people.

The messages concern not only the local church (the parish, the diocese, Yugoslavia) but also the universal church and the whole world. They have been repeated many times and in many different ways with some variations which seem to have no importance.

The Secrets

There are ten secrets confided to the young people by Our Lady. They are destined to be made known. The tenth secret was revealed to Mirjana on December 25, 1982. She is the only one who knows all ten secrets. The other youngsters know nine, except Vicka, who knows eight. All these numbers are provisional. During the last six months, the young people continually grew in their knowledge of the secrets, going from six or seven up to nine. They do not have the right to make these public until Our Lady gives them permission. They firmly resist pressure brought to bear on them by those who can allege good reasons. These people may posses authority, be able to use persuasion, and be among those who are dear to them.

One of the secrets is that there will be a visible sign left by Our Lady as a proof of the authenticity of the apparitions. It is not known when this will take place or what it will be, but the young people are unanimously certain that it will happen.

In addition to these secrets which are going to be made known, there are personal secrets given to each of the young people for his or her own life. These concern the person individually and are not to be made known any more than Bernadette was to make known similar things said to her.

The apparitions are not affected by place. They have taken place in several localities—the mountain, beside the road, in various houses, in the room of the church. Neither are the apparitions affected by the attitudes of the youngsters—at times there were no apparitions, despite their desires and their prayers. They derive from a free and unforeseeable action beyond the laws of this world.

Phenomena of Light

There have been some unexpected phenomena which took place in different localities and were witnessed by different people. On August 2, 1981, there was a solar phenomenon. At sundown the sun seemed to turn around an axis. It seemed to come close and then retreat from those who saw it. There were about 150 people on the hill of the apparitions. They saw the sun as a great heart as it began to turn. They were filled with fear and began to pray and weep. A few ran away. A minute later, a great heart was seen and, below it, six small hearts (the number of those who behold the apparitions). A little later a luminous cloud came down on the hill of the apparitions. After a little while, the cloud moved off toward the sun which, for its part, began to descend and finally set. This phenomenon lasted about 10 or 15 minutes.

Often there appears on the hill of Križevac, above the Cross, a light in the form of a column (see below, p. 146). Many witnesses from villages quite far away, for instance, Miletina, Čitluk, or Gradina, have seen a luminous feminine figure above the hill of Križevac. The phenomenon has lasted anywhere from a few minutes to a half hour. It has occurred at different times of the day. On several occasions, pilgrims visiting Medjugorje have been able to see it.

At the end of October, 1981, in the place of the first apparition, a large flame suddenly shot up. It lasted 10 or 15 minutes. Several hundred people saw this, including priests and religious. A policeman who was there in order to block access to the hill also saw it. He dug around the place without finding any trace of fire or ashes. The old women of the village, who have spent their whole life at Medjugorje, say that there have never been such occurrences in the area.

The Young People Who See The Apparitions

Who are these six adolescents who say they have seen something which no one else has seen? No group can exist without a leader, a plan of action, and a common objective. This is all the more true when it is a question of a group of children whose age does not lead them to make long-term plans for the future. Their interests are rather directed toward the immediate, and they are usually absorbed by their own little projects, which are nearly always quite individualistic. It is for this reason that the strong cohesiveness and especially the long-term duration of the group at Medjugorje is surprising; all the more so because the factors surrounding them do not encourage them but rather increasingly dissuade them.

When the apparitions began, the ages of the young people were from 11 to 17. Their being together was completely fortuitous. Most of them have no family ties to others in the group. They do not live in the same place nor go to the same school. Their characters, ages, and intellectual capacities are very different. Nothing, or practically nothing, could have induced them to form a bond among themselves rather than with others. One would say that it was mere chance that united them during the vacation. Two of their number live in the town, the others in the village.

When a group of youngsters forms without any apparent reason, the specialists tend to think they are sick. But in our case this explanation is excluded. The youngsters have been examined by doctors, by psychotherapists, and other specialists sometimes called in to decide in favor of committing them. All were constrained to declare the youngsters to be in good health. The specialists who examined them were all fiercely opposed to any visions or apparitions, but they had to acknowledge the mental health of the young people.

Another significant observation: the youngsters are bound together in a solid friendship. They do not argue among themselves. They have great respect for one another. There is no rivalry or jealousy, even though they are different in character, intelligence, and culture. They have the good qualities and defects characteristic of their age and place of origin. All of this does not favor their aptitude for forming a group. Nevertheless, they remain closely bound to one another and regularly meet without setting up a rendezvous.

Something else gathers them together besides normal ways of relating. Ivan Ivanković and Milka Pavlović, two who saw the apparition the first day, were not there for any of the other apparitions and do not belong to the group. Nevertheless, Milka is the sister of Marija, who does belong to the group. Later, Ivan and Milka went several times to the place of the apparitions. They retain very friendly relations with the whole group, but they do not belong to it. But this has never been a subject of dispute or jealousy. The only reason why Milka and Ivan do not belong to the group is that they were absent the day of the second apparition. Only the six young people of the second day make up the group. It is obvious, then, that the reason for the formation of the group and for its continuance is not to be found in the group itself but in some external cause.

Before the apparitions, the young people of the group were in no way different from the other young people of the parish, either by reason of their piety, their participation in catechism class, or their frequenting of the Sacraments, even less by their asceticism. Even now, they continue to share in the activities, interests, and games of their friends. They dress like everybody else. They do not put on airs, they are neither fanatics nor bigots. Their life does not give evidence of any particular holiness, nor on the other hand of anything objectionable or scandalous. They are simple, polite, and easy to get along with. To put it quite simply, they are normal. Certain people will think that their behavior does not correspond to the high level of the apparitions, it is not perfect enough: it is not sufficient that it be normal. But it would not be just to demand of youngsters that they be saints simply because they have received a great privilege. We must not forget that an apparition is not a recompense for merit or the result of human effort. It is a pure gift given for the sake of the community.

It is true that faith is also a gift. But the gift of faith also depends upon the personal effort of each person. Faith cannot be communicated if the believer does not share in it, because faith is the gift of oneself to God and therefore the place where grace and human effort flow together and meet each other. Here we can remember the words of the Gospel: "From everyone who has been given much, much will be demanded" (Lk. 12:48). Since faith is the personal response of each person to God, it cannot be replaced by anything. The Virgin Mary herself was called to the obedience of faith, which she gave without reserve (Lk. 1:38). It cannot be otherwise for the young people. But faith is a free act. Human liberty always implies the possibility of avoiding the response which God awaits from man. Every person, whether he sees apparitions or not, is responsible for his faith. Faith cannot grow or arrive at its fullness unless a person gives his consent and makes the necessary effort. The charisms, among which the gift of vision should be included, do not automatically confer holiness. The gifts themselves can only provide an opportunity for growth in faith; the believer can choose to profit from them or not.

What can be said with certainty is that the young people from Medjugorje have quite obviously grown in their faith.

The young people do not derive any glory for themselves from the apparitions. If in regard to this special grace they are more favored than their Bishop and their pastor, they never forget that they owe them respect. The Virgin Mary told them that the priests should help them in their life of faith. Very often lay people or priests ask the young people to recommend them to Our Lady. They do this, but they in no way consider themselves superior to others. This behavior is all the more remarkable in that there are many adults who could not do the same.

There has never been any tension in the group or tendency to break it up. Such consistency is rare among youngsters. Each person in the group respects the personal experience and freedom of the others. No one challenges the fact that someone else belongs to the group nor doubts that others can have apparitions which they do not have. They all consider themselves equals and accept the variations in each one's daily lot.

They all have the same firmness in keeping the ten secrets of Our

Lady despite many efforts to get something from them. Neither their parents nor the priests nor the Bishop have obtained anything. The invisible authority which forbade them to speak is stronger than any other. Bishop Žanić made this proposal to them: "Write the secrets on a piece of paper. Put it in an envelope, and I will keep it under guard." But Jakov, the youngest of the group, who was not quite 11 at the time, refused, saying: "I cannot write them."

They share the same basis for their optimism and joyful confidence in the future. The group has remained united despite a great deal of pressure. The authorities tried to frighten them. Others highlighted the social difficulties that their extravagant claims would bring upon themselves and their families. They have decisively refused any bribes. When it comes to the apparitions, they show none of the fragile and easily influenced reactions of children when faced with attractive promises or threats. People admire their courage. They have suffered because of the apparitions; and they have accepted this consciously and joyously, without any regrets. Any effort to dissuade them only strengthens their calm determination to remain faithful to their convictions.

Their force of character is supported by excellent psychological and physical health. Their good sense and their personal experiences are more credible than those of their schoolmates, and are recognized as such. They never have the slightest hesitation or the least doubt concerning the truth of the message which has been communicated to them. They are ready to die rather than doubt it. This is the mainspring of the group, what formed it, what continues it, and what provides its conviction.

The Leader Of The Group

It is impossible to identify anyone as the leader of the group. No adult guides them, no known person inside or outside the group plays the role of leader, and each of the young people freely gives expression to his or her own experience without fear of the others. Without a doubt Vicka is the one who is surest of herself, but she does not exercise any leadership, nor does she claim any. That responsibility does not interest her or the others. The apparitions did not begin with her but with Ivanka. What is more, at the beginning Vicka was more afraid than the others. When she learned from Mirjana and Ivanka that they had seen the Blessed Virgin, she was so panic-stricken that she ran to the village. She only stopped to take off her shoes, probably so that she could run faster, away from that fearful place.

The young people firmly resist any efforts to sidetrack or oppose them. At the news of the apparitions, their families were surprised and displeased. Vicka's mother and grandmother forbade her to speak about them. They were afraid that the whole family would be considered crazy and would become the butt of jokes. In regard to Ivanka, who was the first to see the Virgin, her parents were not there. Her mother was already dead, and her father was away working in West Germany.

One person who might be suspected of instigating or orchestrating the apparitions is the pastor, Fr. Jozo Zovko. But this hypothesis lacks any basis. First of all, Fr. Zovko was only named pastor a few days before the first apparition. He did not know the parish nor did he know the children at all. More than that, at the time of the first apparitions, he was not at Medjugorje but at a meeting in Zagreb.

When he returned to the parish, the news of the apparitions, already known by everybody, was enough to have gathered a crowd on the hill of the apparitions. Fr. Zovko, who has an analytical mind, trained in criticism, did not approve of all this disturbance. He openly turned people away from the "suspect" apparitions, insisting vigorously on the need to pay attention to the Gospel and to practice Christian virtue. He used to repeat: "Nothing can replace the Sacraments and daily prayer, not even apparitions." He was afraid that these unusual occurrences would result in some deviation from the faith.

When he became convinced, after having seen the apparition once, he was quickly removed from scene, condemned to three and a half years in prison. Regardless of this, the apparitions have not stopped. On the contrary, they continue, and the interest they have stirred up has grown. To sum up: Fr. Zovko did not become involved until after the apparitions had begun and rather than favoring them, he was at first opposed to the fact that the youngsters were forming a group.

Fr. Zrinko Cuvalo, the assistant pastor of Medjugorje, was also suspected of being the one who created the group. But this hard-headed man, skeptical in regard to any innovations in the life of the Church, openly opposed what he considered a fantasy on the part of the youngsters. Whenever anyone spoke to him about it, he shrugged his shoulders and took refuge in the garden. "Here at least," he said, "I am doing something useful. If any want to believe, then let them believe, but I can't believe in it."

When it was obvious that something was happening, he gathered the people, not on the hill of the apparitions, but in the church in order to celebrate Mass and hear confessions. In this he was but performing his duty as shepherd. When he took the place of Fr. Zovko, the pastor who had been put in prison, all of his efforts were directed to bringing the believers back to reason, preaching to them the duties and the truths which are guaranteed by the teaching of the Church. His first refusal to admit the apparitions was providential. He obliged the parishioners and the youngsters to be clearer about what they were saying, and his insistent command of, "Pay attention to the one thing necessary," was not lost. He thus channeled the apparitions into that essential activity of the Mass and the Sacraments.

Just like Thomas, the doubter at the resurrection, Fr. Zrinko played a providential role by resisting. His behavior forced people to make the necessary discernment. So far was he from being the promoter of the apparitions that the political authorities asked that he be named pastor to replace Fr. Zovko, hoping that he would "liquidate" the apparitions. Later he disappointed them and was transferred. This was a relief for him because the unusual situation and the exhausting work that it entailed made him uneasy in a way that he could not overcome. He asked the Bishop either to transfer him or to give him several priests to help him face up to the very demanding situation. When he did not receive the help, he willingly left Medjugorje far behind. His departure changed nothing regarding the specific nature of the group.

With the exception of those who have just been considered, no one else could possibly have been the founder or the guide for the group of youngsters. The priests who are actually in charge of the parish now were far from Medjugorje when the apparitions began; all arrived later. The present pastor, Fr. Tomislav Pervan, came a year after the apparitions began. His assistant, Fr. Tomislav Vlašić, arrived shortly before that. When the apparitions began, he was still at Čapljina (18 miles from Medjugorje).

The Cohesiveness Of The Group

The existence of any group is based upon a common interest to which everything else is subordinated. But the members of this group do not have any personal interest in common. They are too different in age, culture, background, and so forth.

The group can only maintain itself at the cost of some sacrifice. But the young people are not looking for personal gain. The apparitions have taught them the meaning of renunciation. Sometimes people who ask them to pray for them or to transmit their requests to Our Lady offer to give them some money. They never accept this and refuse the money energetically: "Give the alms to the Church." They do not look for thanks or compliments. Neither do their parents, though this situation could have helped to resolve many material problems in the family.

On the eve of every important feast day, the young people keep a strict fast of dry bread and water. Their example has been followed by others. Many people, along with the youngsters themselves, have learned the value of fasting despite hard work in the fields. The Franciscan religious community imitates their example. They fast twice a week, Wednesday and Friday. On these days the young people are particularly strict. They will not even take a cup of black coffee, as others do, to get a little energy.

The difficulties which arise are an incentive for them to go beyond themselves. Threats have never been able to make them retract their affirmation that they have seen the Virgin Mary or to modify the message. They have known what it means to pay the price for this firmness, and the village has learned as well.

What gathers them together is solely the *Blessed Virgin Mary*. The existence of the group and the behavior of the young people have no other explanation. The young people themselves say that the Virgin's authority takes precedence over human authority. Her authority respects their liberty. There is no constraint imposed from above which stifles their personality. Each one is guided in keeping with his or her own temperament, as different as each one is. Their personality traits are not done away with but rather encouraged, elevated, ennobled, and brought to fulfillment. As they give themselves to this training, the young people maintain their personality while remaining part of a coherent group. Their confidence in the future does not reside in the thoughtlessness of youth but rather in the profound conviction that their destiny is in the hands of Our Lady. They do not look on the difficulties which have come to them because of the apparitions as a burden. Their affection for Our Lady makes them light.

Mary guides them with her counsels, but she does this for each one separately. She does not give orders. The young people take her desires very seriously, but they do not commit themselves blindly or to more than they can do. Each one lets his decision come from maturity and faith. There is among them no oath or collective commitment. The decisions are personal. In response to their question, the Virgin expressed the desire that they choose the priestly or religious life, but, she added, only if they themselves desire to do it. Vicka has already made a decision in this direction, and so has Ivan. The others are waiting, and they feel free. They do not decide anything on will power. Rather, they consider the obstacles and the objections. They pray fervently to see things more clearly. They go to Mass and Communion nearly every day. They are aware that Mary is their Mother, but a Mother who is in no way possessive. They always eagerly await the time of their meeting with her.

Mary's teaching is expressed in messages, advice, and recommendations which concern them personally. When the message concerns the whole world, they all hear it, but when it is a counsel or a correction addressed to one among them, only the one intended hears it. When there is a really difficult reprimand, the others can guess it from the reaction.

The young people are at the service of Our Lady. It is in reference to her that they define their group. It is to the Virgin alone that they accord the right to speak to and to guide them as a group. This is the reason, as well, why they never try to find out what the other one has seen or said. This makes the homogeneity of the message all the more striking.

In the objectives of the group there is nothing materialistic, shabby, or superficial. They only desire to transmit to the world the message of Our Lady: peace, faith, repentance, conversion, and prayer. They do not say if their group will continue or not after the apparitions. In this matter as in others, they do not go ahead of the Virgin's plans.

How Those Who Have Seen
The Apparitions Speak About Them

Eight young people at Medjugorje have seen the Virgin Mary. However, two of them, Ivan Ivanković and Milka Pavlović, saw only the first apparition of June 24, 1981. They did not speak to Our Lady, and they do not belong to the group any longer, though Milka, Marija's sister, still shows a certain calm and quiet nostalgia. We questioned only those six who have seen the apparition daily since June 25, 1981. Their answers are below.

Why did the Virgin Mary choose just these six young people and not others? Was it of design that they lived in different villages so that their witness would reach different milieux? Was it so that the credibility and authenticity of the apparitions would be thereby better established? It is difficult to foresee how long the apparitions, which have been going now for more than two years, will last. Does the fact that the apparitions have gone on for so long have anything to do with the tragic situation of our world today, in which there is such a great danger of war? Is this duration necessary so that the world might understand the menace that overshadows it?

The familiarity the young people have with the Blessed Virgin is remarkable. She is their Mother; they are her children. She often calls them "my children" or "my angels" (*andjeli moji*—this expression in Croatian has an intimate and tender connotation that cannot be expressed in English).

I questioned each of the young people very carefully twice, except for Ivanka Ivanković and Ivan Dragicević, whom I questioned but once. Most of the time their answers were identical. The differences arose because of shades of interpretation or where their answers were colored by something the Virgin had said to them personally. Every time that they come together, the Virgin comes to see them, but they spend the rest of their life far from one another. Despite the messages addressed to each one personally, the convergence of their answers is perfect, as is the mutual understanding which prevails among them. Though their fundamental perception is the same, each one receives it according to his temperament. The transcription below of their answers shows in its monotony that they took no care to compose "clever" answers but rather to say what they saw.

Each of the young people is designated by a number, 1-6.

1. Marija Pavlović
2. Jakov Čolo
3. Vicka Ivanković
4. Ivanka Ivanković
5. Mirjana Dragicević
6. Ivan Dragicević

Who taught you that Our Lady exists?

1. I don't know. It must have been my parents or my grandmother.
2. The Franciscan Fathers.
3. I heard about her when I was little. My parents told me that God and Our Lady exist.

4. My grandmother.
5. My parents.
6. My parents and the priests.

Have you seen the Virgin Mary?

1. Yes.
2. Yes.
3. Yes.
4. Yes.
5. Now, never before.
6. Yes.

When did you see Our Lady?

1. June 25, 1981 (*did not come the first day*).
2. June 25, 1981 (*did not come the first day*).
3. June 24, 1981.
4. June 24, 1981.
5. June 24 of last year (*the question was asked in 1982*).
6. June 24, 1981.

Where did you see Our Lady?

1. On the hill of apparitions which is called Crnica.
2. Up there, on our hill Crnica.
3. On the hill of apparitions. We call it Podbrdo. . . . the others call it Crnica.
4. On the hill of Crnica.
5. On the hill of Crnica.
6. On the hill of Crnica.

On the first day of the apparitions, were you sad or sick, or in good health?

1. I was in good health.
2. I was not sick.
3. I was neither sick nor sad.
4. We were happy.
5. Neither one or the other. Medium, normal.
6. I was in good health.

Did you ever want to see Our Lady?

1. It never even crossed my mind.
2. No.
3. Never!
4. Never!
5. It never even crossed my mind. I didn't think that such a thing could happen.
6. I never thought of such a possibility.

How do you know that which you saw was Our Lady?

1. I only understood it later, after the apparitions which followed. I knew because of what people said to me and because of pictures that she is the most beautiful of women.
2. We were at Marija's house, busy at work, and all of a sudden Vicka came running and said, "There she is!" Right away we all left for the hill, running, and at the top we prayed and wept.
3. I saw about two or three hundred yards away, the silhouette of a young woman. She had something in her hands. Mirjana and Ivanka were saying: "Look, Our Lady!" She had a crown of stars and then we thought that it was Our Lady.
4. All of a sudden I looked in the direction of the hill, and I saw something shining. I looked more closely, and then I saw the silhouette of Our Lady. I said to Mirjana: "Look, Our Lady!" She answered: "Let's go. Why do you think Our Lady would appear to us?" So we went home. We went back again with Milka in order to look for the sheep, and I said to them: "Look!" It was really Our Lady. She held Jesus in her arms. I saw the crown on her head, a beautiful long robe, and her hand passed over the head of the child, like this.
5. It was as though someone were saying to me: "It is Our Lady!" I was sure that it was Our Lady.

6. We asked her, and she confirmed it.

Were you afraid when you saw Our Lady?

1. Perhaps the first day we were a little nervous, but our hearts were at peace.
2. I was afraid.
3. The first day I was afraid, and when they called me, I ran away. Then I asked Ivan to come with me, but then he ran away, too. I never imagined that such a thing could happen, and that is why I got out of there. The first day . . . we all screamed and were making faces. The third day I brought along some salt and some holy water, and I said: "If you are Our Lady, stay with us. If not, leave us." Then she smiled.
4. The first day I was afraid, but at the same time I was happy; nevertheless, I was afraid.
5. I was afraid. We girls fainted.
6. Yes, but we didn't dare do anything. The first day we were all afraid. The second day, when we had gone up, we were all moved. The third day we began to feel more at ease.

What did Our Lady look like?

1. She had a gray robe, a white veil, a crown of stars, blue eyes, and black hair.
2. When we saw her the first time, we didn't see very well, she was far away. The second time, when we were close to her, she had a gray robe, a white veil, blue eyes, black hair, rosy cheeks, and she was like this, above the ground.
3. She had a gray robe, white veil, a crown of stars, blue eyes, black hair, rosy cheeks—she was like this, above the ground. On the left, her hair was out from under the veil, you could see that it was curly. She seemed to be very happy, smiling.
4. I can't find the words to describe the beauty of her face. Blue eyes, black hair, which came out a little from under her veil. She was neither tall nor short, about 19 or 20 years old, with a gray robe, white veil, and a crown of stars.
5. The first day she was far from us, and we could only make out her shape. It was as though she held something in her

hands . . . she was very beautiful, a supernatural beauty! I looked at her eyes, which have a marvelous beauty, clear blue. They gazed so gently, with such a goodness! It was wonderful, really! Her face was white with rosy cheeks. You could make out her curly black hair under the veil. Her robe too, so beautiful, like the sky, a little like that.

6. A beautiful face, happy, blue eyes. You couldn't see her hair.

Is Our Lady always dressed in the same way?

1. Always.
2. Yes.
3. Yes, except on the big feast days, for example, August 15, September 8, Christmas, Easter, the Immaculate Conception, she has golden clothing, shining, different. But the other days, always the same.
4. Yes.
5. No, she is always dressed in a gray robe, but on special occasions, for the Assumption, then Our Lady had a marvelous robe that was all shining.
6. Yes.

How do you see her?

1. Like a person.
2. A living being.
3. Like you, right now, the same. A living being.
4. Like a human being.
5. Like you right now as I talk to you. I can touch her.
6. Like you.

Does Our Lady appear right away, or is there something that precedes her?

1. There is a light, like a flash of lightning three times. Then it is Our Lady.
2. First, a light appears. Before, it used to come three times. Now there is just one light. The light appears; then Our Lady comes.
3. Beforehand there is a light which appears three times, and then Our Lady.

4. Light.
5. Light.
6. Light.

How did you get the idea of going back to the hill where Our Lady appeared the first time?

1. Something drew us; we don't know what, certainly some power from God.
2. Well, something drew me there.
3. Ivanka suggested a walk toward the hill of the apparition, and if we were to see Our Lady, so much the better, and if we were not to see her, we would keep quiet so that others wouldn't make fun of us.
4. One of us said: "Let's go back to the mountain. Our Lady was there yesterday; maybe she will appear there today."
5. I had the impression that I ought to go there. Something told me that I ought to go to the hill.
6. We went to see if Our Lady hadn't left a sign on the hill of the apparition.

Has Our Lady appeared in several places?

1. On the hill of the apparitions; it also happened here, in our houses, in the parish church.
2. Up there on our hill, at home, in the fields; now she appears in the church.
3. On the hill of the apparitions, at home, in the church. She appeared where we were.
4. On the hill, in houses, in our houses, and in nearly all the others, in the fields, in the church.
5. On the hill, in the church, in the chapel beside the Cross, and in the choir, in my room. Wherever I was, she was with me.
6. On the hill, in the houses, in the church, here in the chapel.

Have you touched Our Lady?

1. Yes, I touched her robe; each time I touched it, it was with my whole palm. Many also touched her.
2. Yes, I touched her robe.

3. Yes, I touched her robe, but it is resistant like metal. I want to say that when she moves her hands or head, she moves, that's normal; but when you touch, there is resistance, like metal.
4. Yes.
5. I can touch her. . . . At the beginning, I looked on her as something inaccessible, but now, when she is with me, I look on her as a Mother, as my best friend, who helps me.
6. I touched her robe.

Did you say to anyone that Our Lady appeared to you?

1. Yes, I said it to many people. I said it to everyone who asked me.
2. The first time, I told my mother.
3. Yes, down there, on the road, they asked me: "What's going on?" I told them: "I saw Our Lady!"
4. I spoke to my grandmother, and she told me: "Come, now, it was somebody watching sheep who had put a flashlight on his head." Afterwards, Vicka also spoke to her mother, and they made fun of us.
5. We told our family, but the word got around quickly.
6. To our parents and neighbors.

What did they say?

1. Those first days, everyone was curious, and they were always asking questions. Now, there are also people who come and ask questions.
2. My mother didn't believe me.
3. They began to joke. They asked me: "And did Our Lady say hello to your grandmothers?" Nobody believed, and they all made fun.
4. They made fun of us.
5. They rather believed me. At least for me I can say this.
6. They found all this strange; and they didn't believe at first that Our Lady had appeared.

What did you do when the others didn't believe?

1. I was peaceful. Afterwards I prayed for their conversion.

2. Well, nothing. I didn't want to get mixed up in something.

3. I smiled, that's all. They couldn't influence me no matter what they said or didn't say.

4. At first, I was really troubled; even now sometimes that troubles me. Maybe I would have reacted the same way. But since I had faith, why wouldn't I believe? Many have been converted. Now they're more apt to believe than before.

5. I took it as though they believed me. If they didn't believe, that was their personal affair. I wasn't annoyed in any way.

6. I would have preferred that they believe but, if they didn't want to, that was their personal affair.

Did you tell the pastor that Our Lady had appeared to you?

1. First we told the assistant pastor. When the pastor came, we went back and told him as well. He didn't say yes or no; he didn't encourage us. Nothing. We went back home, and it was later that the pastor began to question us.

2. The first time we spoke to him, he said nothing.

3. The pastor was at Zagreb. Fr. Zrinko was there, and he said: "He who has the gift to see, let him look; he who doesn't have the gift isn't obliged."

4. Yes. When Fr. Jozo arrived, he came to look for us. We told him how it happened.

5. He only listened to us. He didn't say anything else to us.

6. We went to find the pastor, but Fr. Jozo wasn't home. He was at Zagreb on a retreat. We spoke to another [priest]. He said: "I don't understand." The first day he wasn't inclined to believe. Then Fr. Jozo came. He said: "Pray!"

How did Our Lady introduce herself?

1. The Blessed Virgin Mary.
2. The Blessed Virgin Mary.
3. I am the Blessed Virgin Mary.
4. I am the Blessed Virgin Mary.
5. The Blessed Virgin Mary.
6. I am the Blessed Virgin Mary.

What language did she speak?

1. Our language! Croatian.
2. Croatian.
3. Everything in Croatian.
4. Croatian.
5. Croatian.
6. Croatian.

What does Our Lady say at the beginning of her meeting with you?

1. Praised be Jesus.
2. Praised be Jesus.
3. Praised be Jesus.
4. Praised be Jesus.
5. Praised be Jesus.
6. Praised be Jesus.

Who speaks first, Our Lady or you?

1. She does.
2. When she comes, she says: "Praised be Jesus!" Afterwards, I ask her that which I have to ask her.
3. She does.
4. She does.
5. She does.
6. She does.

How long will Our Lady keep appearing?

1. I don't know.
2. We asked her that once, and she said to us: "Is it that you've had enough of me?" Now we don't want to ask her anymore.
3. She never said. Once when we asked her, she said: "Is it that you've had enough of me?"
4. We don't know.
5. I don't know exactly.
6. I don't know.

Can you determine the time of Our Lady's appearing?

1. We cannot.
2. We cannot.
3. We cannot.
4. We can't know when.
5. Not in such a rude way. We make an agreement among ourselves. Today I make an agreement with her as to when she can appear the next day.
6. We cannot.

Can you foretell with certainty when Our Lady is going to appear?

1. Well, sometimes we were sure that she was going to appear to us, and nevertheless she never appeared that day.
2. We cannot. We pray that she comes.
3. I think so. But I cannot know it with certainty.
4. As for me, I do it this way. I have a sense that she will come, but I cannot know with certainty.
5. She always tells us when she will come. If she doesn't say it, I have a sense.
6. We cannot.

Why did Our Lady appear to you? Is it because you're nicer than other people?

1. I don't know.
2. I don't know.
3. She said that she doesn't always look for the best.
4. She said that it's not always necessary to look for the best.
5. She said that she never looks for the best.
6. I don't know, but I don't think it's because I'm better than others.

Does she appear to you because you're better than others?

1. I am not.
2. I am not.
3. No.
4. I don't think so.

5. I am not.
6. I am not.

Does it cause you joy that Our Lady appears to you?

1. Oh, it is an inexpressible joy!
2. Of course it makes for joy.
3. Yes, it makes for joy. How could it be otherwise?
4. Yes.
5. Yes.
6. Yes.

How long do the apparitions last?

1. Sometimes more, sometimes less; five, ten, fifteen minutes.
2. Sometimes five, sometimes ten minutes, sometimes a half hour.
3. That depends. Sometimes five, sometimes ten minutes, sometimes fifteen or twenty minutes. That depends on Our Lady.
4. Here where I live, five or six minutes, and before, we had it for about a half hour. For me personally at Mostar, also a half hour, never less than fifteen minutes.
5. About a half hour; fifteen minutes or ten.
6. That depends: five, ten, fifteen to twenty minutes.

Do other persons besides Our Lady appear to you?

1. Yes. One time we saw Jesus. In one appearance, Our Lady told us that she would show us, as it were, an image of Jesus covered with wounds. We saw him that way. This took place in one of our houses.
2. Yes. Jesus. In Ivanka's house. He was covered with blood. He was wearing the crown of thorns.
3. She showed us Jesus when we were in a house, Ivanka's. He seemed to be tall. He had the crown of thorns. His eyes . . . he looked up, like this. She showed him to us, and she said: "This is so that you might see how my Son suffers in all humanity."

4. We saw the head of Jesus. It was at my house. Our Lady said: "This is my Son, bruised for the world."

5. Once I saw behind Our Lady the head of Jesus. It was during the examination by Dr. and Mrs. Dzuda at Mostar.

6. Yes.

Have you seen anything else besides Our Lady and Jesus?

1. We saw heaven, hell, and purgatory. Our Lady showed us this also. Once, here at Vicka's house, once at my house, and another time, but I don't remember where. I saw heaven, like people who were so happy; no, I can't describe that beauty. In fact, you see that the love of God is there. And hell, where people suffer and are in pain: it's something horrible.

2. The angels, at Vicka's house.

3. When Jozo (the pastor) was in prison, once Our Lady showed him to us. It was like a movie. We have seen heaven and hell. There is a great space. In heaven there are many people, and when you enter . . . on the left there is a man. I didn't ask any questions about him, who he is or what he does. He opens the door. The people are smiling and praying. Up above the angels are soaring. In hell, in the middle there is a huge fire. There are no coals—nothing, just the flames. Many people go, one by one, crying. . . . May God protect us from it!

4. I also saw two angels, my mother, hell, and heaven.

5. Yes. Once I saw the devil. I was waiting for Our Lady and, just at the moment when I wanted to make the sign of the Cross, he appeared to me in her place. Then I was very afraid. He promised me all the beautiful things of the world, but I said no! Then, all of a sudden, he disappeared, and Our Lady appeared. She told me that he always tries to turn the true believer from the right path. Our Lady showed me heaven. It is wonderful there. Everybody is happy, joyful. In every face you can see that they are happy. . . . the trees, the meadows, the sky, are all completely different from ours, the sun too, which is much more brilliant. What I saw impressed me.

6. Jesus.

Did Our Lady confide any secrets to you?

1. Yes. I know six secrets. The others know seven or eight. They have to do with us, the Church, people in general.
2. Yes. They have to do with our life and with people.
3. Yes. I have seven. The first secret has to do with our church at Medjugorje. It has to do as well with the sign, humanity in general, and each person. The secrets speak of the Church in general. There are some which concern us.
4. Yes. I have seven. Some concern us personally, others, the Church and the world.
5. Nine secrets were confided to me. They have to do with us ourselves, the [final] sign, the whole world, and also Medjugorje.
6. Yes.

(These answers were true at the time of the questioning, the beginning of December, 1982. At Christmas, December 25, Mirjana received the tenth secret. The others know nine, except Vicka, who knows eight.)

Does Our Lady have a message for the world?

1. All the secrets concern the world. There are also messages - peace, faith, conversion, prayer, fasting, repentance.
2. People have to pray and fast. We have to be converted and foster peace.
3. She said: prayer, penance, conversion, peace; the most important message is peace. She insisted on that.
4. Our Lady said that the most important thing is to have a strong faith. We should pray every day, at least saying seven times the Our Father, Hail Mary, Glory Be to the Father, and the Creed. It is necessary to do penance, and every Friday to eat nothing but dry bread and drink nothing but water.
5. She said that prayer, faith, and fasting are very important. With these means it is possible to stop wars and prevent catastrophes. Both of these are very frequent today.
6. We should be converted to the faith, make it stronger and deeper so that it can be passed on from one generation to the next.

Did Our Lady leave a special message for priests?

1. She said to priests that they should safeguard their faith. But I can't remember exactly now.
2. She said to them to safeguard the faith of their people.
3. She said only that priests should preserve the faith of their people.
4. I don't remember.
5. She said to the priests of Medjugorje that they should accept us.
6. That they should keep and spread the faith.

Did Our Lady have a message for the Bishop?

1. There is a message for the Bishop. We went up there right away, and we told it to him. I know it [the message] more or less, but he told us not to speak to anyone about it.
2. That he persevere.
3. Yes, but I cannot because he said that it is only for him and that we should not speak about it to others.
4. She said something, I don't remember now exactly what.
5. No, except when he was at Mostar and when I asked about him. This concerns nobody but him.
6. That he carry out his duties regularly.

Did Our Lady have a message for the Pope?

1. I don't know.
2. She told it to Vicka.
3. That he should consider himself as the father of all people and not only the Christians. That he tirelessly and courageously promote the message of peace and love for all men. This is found among the secrets that she gave us, but we shouldn't speak about it now, only when she permits us to say it. There is a little of everything.
4. I can't tell you everything, only that he should extend the faith to all people because we are more or less equal and that he persevere on his path.
5. No.
6. No.

Are you authorized to divulge the secrets to others?

1. No. Our Lady told us that we could not divulge these secrets.
2. We don't have the right because she hasn't told us to.
3. No. We don't have the right because she hasn't told us to.
4. No, to no one.
5. No.
6. No.

Do the secrets speak about good or ill for the world?

1. Well, that's a secret.
2. There is some good and some bad as well.
3. There is good and bad.
4. There are some things that are good, and there are some things that are bad.
5. There are some nice things and some unpleasant things.
6. There are some things that are good, and there are some things that are bad.

When will Our Lady permit you to divulge the secrets?

1. I don't know. She will tell us when, what, and to whom.
2. I don't know.
3. When she tells us.
4. I don't know.
5. She hasn't told us yet.
6. When she agrees.

Has she promised to do something to show to others that it really is Our Lady?

1. Our Lady has promised to leave a sign for those who do not believe.
2. Yes. She will leave a great sign.
3. She said that she will leave a great sign.
4. Yes. Our Lady said that she will leave a great sign on the hill of the apparitions.
5. Yes.
6. Yes.

When will Our Lady give this sign?

1. That also is a secret.
2. We know, but we don't have the right to reveal it.
3. I don't know. I don't have the right to tell.
4. That's not important.
5. It's one of the secrets.
6. It's a secret.

The sign which Our Lady has promised, will it be visible for everyone?

1. It will.
2. It will.
3. It will.
4. Absolutely.
5. Yes.
6. Yes.

When will the sign appear?

1. That also is a secret.
2. We know, but we don't have the right to reveal it.
3. I know. Oh, but I don't have the right to tell. I would like to tell.
4. I know.
5. I cannot tell.
6. It's a secret.

Did Our Lady ask you to say a special prayer?

1. She told us that it was best to recite the Creed and to sing the song: "O Christ, in your name we are here, for we believe that you are with us. Without you we are weak . . . Give us strength."
2. Seven times the Our Father, Hail Mary, and Glory Be to the Father, and the Creed once.
3. No, nothing special: the Rosary, seven times the Our Father, Hail Mary, Glory Be to the Father, and the Creed.
4. She said that she prefers the Creed and the song, "O Christ, in your name . . ." When we wish to meet with her, we recite the Our Father, and she comes.

5. She recommended to us to pray for those who are in purgatory.
6. Seven times the Our Father, Hail Mary, Glory Be to the Father, and the Creed.

Who first suggested to you to recite seven times the Our Father, Hail Mary, Glory Be to the Father, and the Creed?

1. I don't know.
2. It was Mirjana's grandmother who first gave her this advice. Then we all recited them in front of Our Lady, and she told us to continue to recite this prayer.
3. First of all, Mirjana's grandmother told her to recite seven Our Father's, . . .then, when we had arrived up there, Mirjana began to recite seven Our Father's, and we followed her. Then Our Lady told us to continue to recite this prayer.
4. Mirjana's grandmother advised us to say this prayer.
5. We recited it the first time in front of Our Lady. She told us that pleased her and to continue to recite that prayer.
6. It was an old woman, a grandmother, who gave us that advice, and Our Lady told us to continue to recite that prayer.

Did our Lady tell you what you should do in life?

1. She proposed to us to enter religious life, if we wanted to. She said that was what she wanted.
2. Her desire is that we all enter religious life.
3. Once she said to us: "I would wish that you become nuns and priests, but I do not wish to oblige anyone."
4. Our Lady said to us: "If you should wish to become nuns, that would be my wish as well. But if you do not wish it, then it is better not to do it." She said: "On condition that we can and that we desire to, but not to enter and then leave; to bring dishonor on the church and everyone!"
5. We told her only that some among us desire to become nuns or Franciscan friars, and that the others wished to continue their life as it is now. She said that was our affair. She said that both the one and the other were good. She explained and gave her advice.

6. I asked her if I should become a priest. She said to me: "That is for you to decide."

So what have you decided?

1. Well, at that same instant I made the decision to enter the convent.
2. I decided to go there [to the monastery].
3. I decided to become a nun.
4. I don't want to enter the convent.
5. To continue school. Afterwards, I will see.
6. I decided to become a priest.

Do you go out with anybody?

1. No.
2. Yes, a little. I watch T.V. a little, only when there is a movie.
3. No.
4. I go out.
5. Yes.
6. No.

Do you prefer to enter religious life or to marry?

1. To enter religious life.
2. To enter religious life.
3. To enter religious life.
4. To get married. I don't know what I will decide after a few years.
5. I don't know.
6. To enter religious life.

Have the apparitions changed anything for you?

1. I have changed in many respects: my whole life has changed. Between "before" and "after," everything is different from every point of view. Every day I try to be better. Now I go to church with more pleasure. I also like prayer more and to go to Communion more than before.

2. Yes. Now I go regularly to Mass. I pray regularly. I am more obedient. I have more pleasure in praying and in going to Communion.

3. Before, at Mass I used to wait for the end. Yes, I've completely changed. I pray more. Before, I hurried through my prayers. Now I love to go to church.

4. I pray more. I used to pray before, but I have more power today. I think I have become better. Now I go to church with more pleasure. I rather like to pray, to go to confession and to Communion.

5. Yes. I believe more. Now I attend Mass with more attention, and I understand better. I love to go to church, to pray, to go to confession more than before.

6. My life is changed. I wish to become a priest. I have decided to follow this path. I pray more.

Does Our Lady perform miracles? Has she healed people?

1. There are many healings through the intercession of Our Lady.

2. Yes.

3. She heals people.

4. Yes.

5. Yes.

6. Yes.

Do you know any of the people who were healed?

1. Yes, I know many of them. They came with us today, and I saw them. Often they come from far away. Right here there is only little Danijel, who lives close. He comes sometimes.

2. I know them. There are many.

3. I know 20 or 30, but I don't know their names. I've forgotten. The office at the presbytery keeps track.

4. There are many. Myself for example. I know others, but I don't know their names, except Danijel Sětka from Vukodol near Mostar, a three-year-old child, paralyzed. He was little, and he could neither speak nor walk, and it was right here in the church that he began to speak and walk.

5. There have been many.

6. Yes, there are many.

What does Our Lady ask of people before healing them?

1. She always asks faith, prayer, fasting.

2. She asks prayer, penance, conversion, peace.

3. Above all she asks for a strong faith.

4. Strong faith and prayer.

5. Only strong faith, prayer, and fasting.

6. Prayer, penance, faith.

Did Our Lady recommend that you go to Mass and Communion?

1. Yes.

2. Yes.

3. Certainly! Communion and Mass—she insisted on this.

4. No, never.

5. Yes.

6. Yes.

Has Our Lady ever reprimanded you?

1. Sometimes. If we've done something that isn't right, she reprimands us right away. She tells us that we have to change our behavior, that we have to correct this or that action. Sometimes Our Lady has given me advice, and in some particular situations when I could not see how to resolve them, it was she who told me what I ought to do.

2. Sometimes, not often.

3. Me, never! She only corrected a word that I did not have the right to say.

4. As for me, she hasn't found fault with me.

5. She said that I was too naive, that I ought to correct that. I believe everybody too much.

6. Yes.

Are you tired of Our Lady's apparitions?

1. I am never tired of them.

2. No.

3. Not at all.

4. No.

5. No.

6. No.

Can you swear what you have said is true?

1. I can.

2. I can.

3. Not once but a hundred times!

4. Certainly, I can!

5. I can, naturally!

6. I can!

The Queen of Peace

"I am the Queen of Peace." This is how the apparition described herself to the young people. This title sums up all her messages. When we look at them closely, we find that peace is always at the center. Our Lady is inviting us to a radical peace. Peace is the root; conversion, prayer, and fasting flow from it, expressing faith and putting us in touch with salvation. Salvation itself is nothing else but peace, *shalom*, the high point of all the messianic promises and of the whole work of Christ.

Fr. Petar Ljubičić said to the youngsters: "Ask for her name. We know that she is Our Lady, but she is coming under another title and, without a doubt, with another name. What is it?" "She wanted to tell us the name. Your question has already been answered. She said, 'I am the Queen of Peace'. We were at Jakov's house that day. Those are her exact words."

Fr. Zrno of Chicago asked if the Virgin Mary had revealed anything about herself, as at Lourdes. The assistant pastor, Fr. Tomislav Vlašić, did not know how to answer. This was just before the 6:00 p.m. Mass that he was going to say himself. After the Mass little Jakov ran up, not knowing that Fr. Zrno and Fr. Vlašić had been speaking just before Mass. He gave them a little piece of paper on which was written: "There are many who have asked my name: I am the Queen of Peace." This was Our Lady's answer to the two priests. It was given on August 6, 1981.

The word "peace" was written in shining letters in the sky. All those who were out of doors at the time and who looked in that direction could see it. I asked many people at Gradnic and Bijakovići about this. They all confirmed it. Others could also see it, and they declared: "We saw it." Everyone saw this sign at the same time. It was so well known that Fr. Jozo Zovko spoke about it at the Mass he celebrated after the event.

The physical and spiritual healings for which the pilgrims to Medjugorje give thanks are a sign of the authenticity of the apparitions.

Father Rupčić's Conclusion

These are the essential facts up to the date of this writing. We have seen the physical and psychological health of the young people, their honesty, the good influence that the events have had on their life of faith, which has become more intense and based on the Gospel itself. The revelations they have received have a prophetic nature. They are words addressed to our world in the name of God.

This prophetic grace will not be completely clear until the secrets are divulged and the sign, about which we are still ignorant, is known. The important thing for the moment is that these prophecies are founded on the fact that God is the master of history and the future and that he is stirring men to belief and to conversion. These are not the promises of a rosy future. We are still on earth where we must carry the Cross. The prophecies are in accord with revelation, and they in no way contradict it.

Obviously we are talking about personal revelations which cannot be put on the same level as the universal revelation made to the whole Church. These actualize essential elements of that revelation for our time. They are given without any impression of an automatic outcome or magic. At Medjugorje Our Lady is appearing in her glory as the Servant of the Lord, to whom Jesus confided the human race at the foot of the Cross. She is fulfilling that role. She is inviting us freely to cooperate with her, to be available. Her approach is not that of a judge. She is encouraging, comforting, entreating, like a mother: the Mother of all.

She does not wish to take a person's place or to tell them exactly what they have to do. Rather, she is addressing herself to each one's free will as this is sustained by the grace and light of God. At Medjugorje Our Lady wakes the sleepy, comforts the weak, gives heart to the discouraged, consoles the desperate, and leads the wanderers back to the Father's house. She comes with love to serve God in the people of today.

Who Are These Young People?

1. Jakov Čolo, born in Bijakovići on June 3, 1971. His
father, Ante, works in Sarajevo and his mother, Jaca,
died on September 5, 1983. Since her death, Jakov has
been cared for by his uncle Philip Pavlović, a brother of
the deceased. Philip is also the father of Marija. Jakov is
the youngest of the group. He is a good student and is
very lively and mischievous. He likes soccer and music
and plays the harmonium. He has recovered from the

death of his mother with strength, supported by the visits from Mary. He
prefers to stay where he is, and continues to attend school in the village.

2. Ivan Dragicević, born in Bijakovići on May 25, 1965.
He is the son of Stanko, a farmer, and Zlata. After an
unfortunate scholastic venture in the minor seminary
of Dubrovnik, for which the village school had not prepared him, he is continuing his studies prior to entering
the Franciscan order. Quiet and calm, he goes to Mass
every day with his parents and works with them on the
farm. Ivan is the eldest of three children.

Like a good peasant, he is quietly learning to overcome his shyness and
scholastic deficiencies. He is taking correspondence courses and goes to
Zagreb for his exams. He is from a family of strong believers.

3. Mirjana Dragicević, born in Bijakovići on March 18,
1965. She is the daughter of Jozo, an x-ray technician in
a local hospital, and of Milena, who works in a factory.
She has a younger brother named Miroslav. Both are
good students. Mirjana is pursuing studies in agronomy
at the University of Sarajevo. Her visions ended on
December 25, 1982, but the Blessed Virgin promised
that exceptions would be granted in times of crisis and

on her birthday every year. She continues to pray and to receive commun-
ion regularly. She returns to Bijakovići every year to spend her vacation
there.

We should also note:
Ivan Ivanković was born in Bijakovići on January 3, 1960. He is the son of Jozo
and Zdrava Sivric. Ivan saw only the apparition of June 24. He is a lathe
operator in a factory.

4. Ivanka Ivanković, born in Bijakovići on April 21, 1966. She is the daughter of Ivan, who works in West Germany, and Jagoda, who died in May 1981, a month before the apparitions began. She attends secondary school in Mostar, where she lives with her family. Her older brother Martin also attends the secondary school in Mostar. Her sister Daria goes to school with her. The  family has held on to an inherited piece of land in their native village of Bijakovići. They spend their vacations there and farm the land at that time. Ivanka is a regular communicant. She is a great help to her aged grandmother, Iva, who has been taking care of the house since the death of the mother. Ivanka is the only one of the youngsters who plans to get married.

5. Vicka Ivanković was born in Bijakovići on July 3, 1964. Her father's name is Pero. He has been working in West Germany for the past 15 years to provide for the needs of his large family. Her mother's name is Zlata. There are eight children. The older children farm Pero's land and grow tobacco and grapes. The grand-  mother, also named Vicka, is doing well at age 88. Mirjana, Vicka's oldest sister, received her diploma from the College of Pharmacy. She is now married. The second oldest sister completed her studies at the Professional Business School and is now working. She also is married. The younger children are still in grade school. Members of the family are believers and practice their faith. The father is exemplary. Vicka is finishing her studies at the Professional Textile School in Mostar. She spends a lot of time taking care of little Jakov, the orphan. She is preparing to enter religious life.

6. Marija Pavlović, born in Bijakovići on April 1, 1965. Her father, Philip, is a farmer, her mother, Iva, has six children. Marija's three brothers, Pero, Andria, and Ante, work in West Germany. Her sister Ruzica is already married. Her young sister Milka is still in grade school in Bijakovići. Marija is finishing her apprentice-  ship as a hairdresser in Mostar. Calm and determined of character, she has decided to enter religious life, but has not yet set a date, since she is still involved with the apparitions.

Milka Pavlovic, born in Bijakovici on January 3, 1968, is the sister of Marija. She saw the apparition only on the first day, June 24, 1981. Her mother would not let her return the second day. Ever since then, she has had no vision. She remembers, with a touch of nostalgia, but without bitterness.

Vicka, Jakov, Marija and Ivan praying during an apparition.

Jakov and Vicka praying during an apparition.

St. James Church at Medjugorje built by local people between 1937-1969, far surpassing their needs at the time of construction.

Chapter Three

The Apparitions
Since July, 1981

The book published by Fr. Rupčić, of which Chapter Two is the translation and adaptation, restricts itself to the first seven apparitions and a general description of what followed. The apparitions have continued until the date of this writing (September 1984). A visit to Medjugorje at Christmas 1983 (December 23-27) enabled us to take account of the latest developments that further correspondence has brought up to date. I will present, then, four general aspects (the totality of this immense spiritual event, still incomplete, defies comprehensive analysis): 1) The natural and spiritual unfolding of the event; 2) The charisms; 3) The words of the Virgin Mary; and 4) What I saw at Medjugorje (December 24, 25, and 26, 1983).

The Nature And Spiritual Unfolding Of The Event

I ARRIVED AT MEDJUGORJE ON DECEMBER 24, 1983. THE MOST STRIKING aspect of the environment is the uncomplicated and deep fervor with which this peasant parish in an atheistic country lives out its meeting with Our Lady and her message. Conversion, reconciliation, prayer, fasting—these are not empty words. Often those who go to confession have come from a long way off: 20, 30, or 40 years away from the Sacraments. The ongoing development of the events which we are now going to trace is very significant.

The police have been there since the end of June 1981, as we have seen. They interrogated the young people on June 27 and 29. On June 30 the pastor, who was in the church, felt himself moved to go outside in order "to protect the young people." He found them in the hands of the police, getting ready for a third interrogation. He then found a legal means of defending the youngsters. According to the law, the police do not have the right to interrogate minors without the authorization of their parents. The parents made their opposition known, and the interrogations legally ceased. Toward the end of June the young people, still vulnerable to the police, asked Our Lady if she could not appear in the church, the only place where worship is allowed. Access to the hill was being impeded. On July 13 it was closed off by a police blockade. The apparitions retreated to the houses where the young people experienced them individually at times but more often all together at one or other of their houses. The place of meeting was kept secret so that the safety of the owners of the house would not be compromised: reprisal is not an empty word when the government deals with religion. In this country religious worship is strictly confined to the church where it can be easily controlled. Anything exceeding this is liable to sanction.

It was near the beginning of July that the young people asked: "How long are you going to appear?" The Virgin smiled: "Are you already tired of me?" They understood that this implied a long duration.

The pastor, Fr. Jozo Zovko, was not yet convinced. He had been trained to have an analytical mind. During the apparitions he had been at Zagreb for a course of renewal. He was distrustful of irrational supernatural occurrences that defy normal controls and allow a subjective explanation. He made his skepticism known, and he tried to bring the thing back to solid ground. He never ceased repeating: "The essential is faith and the Sacraments."

His own pastoral practice was firmly rooted in this essential. When the apparitions became less public, he began a daily Mass; this was July 2. Each day after the apparition, Mass was celebrated, and the young people came along quite simply. There was a large crowd at these Masses, and prayer was intense. The exceptional supernatural event thus led people to the sacraments. The Virgin was bringing people to the Eucharist, and the pastor began to be troubled by the abundance of conversions and confessions.

Heaven leaned down to this man of God with his austere and analytical intellectualism. One evening in the summer of 1981, the young people who were in the church saw a silent apparition during the ceremony itself. He saw it, too. He was stupefied. He never thought that could happen to him—to him with his common sense and determined practicality.

He became another man. His preaching, which up to that point had been conscientious and boring, took on a new life. It was a fire that drew its nourishment from biblical images eminently suited to this peasant people whom he knew well with their limits and defects. He pricked their faith and their consciences.

However, this new inspiration brought him trouble. One day he was preaching about the journey through the desert: those 40 years during which the people of God wandered between the captivity in Egypt and the entrance into the promised land. It spoke to his audience. However, the police were there keeping his preaching under surveillance: "He said 40 years!" The policeman didn't know that the number was in the Bible. What was obvious to him was that the number 40 corresponded to the 40 years of Marxist regime in Yugoslavia. The sermon was subversive! The police came to the presbytery. On August 17, 1981, Fr. Jozo was arrested and condemned to three and a half years in prison. The daily newspaper *Novosti* (*The News*) accused him of wanting to stir up once again the violent nationalist movement of the Ustaši "in the very place of the crime" (reference to an event at Bijakovići in which some Marxists were killed; also 2,500 local people were killed by Tito's partisans). However, 40,000 letters of protest, addressed to the President of the Republic and sent from Italy during the fall of 1981, obtained the reduction of his sentence to two and a half and then one and a half years; he was released during the summer of 1983.

The weight of the responsibility for the parish fell on his assistant, another Franciscan, Fr. Zrinko Cuvalo, who had the same reservations. He was pastor until August 20, 1982. He was caught in a trap, like the officer of a battalion too enthusiastic for him: "There they go; I have to follow them, I am their leader."

The fruits of grace began to convince him. His pastoral approach was patient, courageous and austere, but the people were ready for anything. The intensity of their collective zeal gave coherence to the movement.

Beginning January 14, 1982, the daily apparition was transferred to the church, not in the nave, but in a small room which is an annex to the sacristy. People of the parish come together in the church to recite the Rosary, which begins about 5:20 p.m. Shortly before 6:00 p.m., the young people go up the stairs which lead to the out-of-the-way place of the apparitions, to the right of the altar. Each day about ten people are allowed to go with them. They are those who have come from a long distance, are there to study the apparitions, or who have asked the youngsters to transmit a particular request. When the apparition is over, the young people finish the prayer behind the altar along with the crowd.

It is not a sentimental prayer. There are no starry-eyed gazes, no tense atmosphere or surface emotion. The prayer which continues in the parish church is peasant prayer, pure and hard like the rocks of the mountain where the apparitions began. The voices are rough without any intonation. They recite the prayer in strong, well carved syllables, almost hammered out. It is really from the soil, as though from a rock, that this prayer goes up to heaven. It goes up like a flame, not smoke. It is not complicated, exaggerated or affected. It is impressive. It seizes you not at an emotional level but in a much deeper area of your being. It is that place where man discovers himself to be indwelt by God, the Creator, who created him to be a man of labor, a rational animal. The body of the animal, its cry, well controlled by the monotonous prayer of the Church, enters into the movement. It is not weakened despite the lack of comfort. Most often half the people must remain standing for a good two hours. The church, which is not heated, is cold in the winter, but it warms up, like a stable, when all the bodies are gathered there. The summer is worse when the gathered crowd concentrates the heat.

My pilgrimage took place amid great austerity. The village is far from any means of transport, any principal railroad line or main road. You arrive there across a bridge whose upper structure has fallen perilously into the river. The government had the Sisters' school demolished—private schools not being authorized by law. The Sisters thus lost their lodging as well and are crowded into the second floor of the presbytery, while the priests live on the ground floor in very cramped quarters. I had to stay at the Hotel Čitluk, about 8 miles away. To help me regain energy during the intensive days of my inquiry, Fr. Tomislav could offer me only the use of his own bed for a short nap while he prayed or worked. The government has not allowed the leveling off of the ruins of the school nor authorized the preparation of a large, open flat place suitable to receive cars or the crowd. These administrative vexations are put up with patiently. I only learned about them, as about many things, because I asked questions and made observations of my own. Mary's message of penance makes the austerity easy to bear. What matters is the prayer which gathers people together despite the lack of comfort.

The Charisms

What I saw at Medjugorje with my eyes, which are not those of a visionary but a theologian more modestly concerned with the evaluation of what can be perceived, is this: the coherent development of a community of faith animated by the various charisms. It is the development of the charisms which will be the subject of this second section.

Those Who Have Seen the Apparitions

At Medjugorje everything has taken its origin from the apparitions. They have been transmitted by the charism of witness which the youngsters have exercised quite well before their priests, their families, their parish, visitors, the police, etc. They bear witness simply, joyfully, they are neither too forward nor too timid. They have seen something. They still see something. They are happy. Their life is growing with God, and there is light in it. The witness in words is but an addition to their constant way of being, each one according to his own temperament. They are very different.

Vicka is a complete extrovert. Her face lights up at the beginning of each apparition with a transparent smile, while her lips form expressive words which no one can hear.

Ivan is serious, almost grave, and quite introverted. This surely must cause him some suffering. He is patient, however, and calm in the resolution of this problem, which has been in large part resolved. Those who look down on his meager scholarly achievements at the Seminary of Dubrovnik, where he first studied, recognize his politeness, his solid piety, his uprightness, even if they don't believe in the apparitions. He has some difficulty coming out of himself, adapting himself to situations, but the fundamental ease of his being is much stronger than the surface inhibitions. There is nothing disagreeable or evasive in his attitude. He used to be a loner, now he is sociable. He used to be fearful, now he has found peace and security. He too is disarming with his tact and simplicity.

Each of the other young people has his or her own temperament: Marija, tactful, receptive, communicative; little Jakov Čolo, brimming with life and energy. He loves to play soccer, but he also plays the harmonium. He gives the impression of absolutely magnificent health and balance. Each of the young people have their own dialogue with the Virgin, his or her own way of relating and receptivity, his or her different mission.

Vicka receives prophetic messages about the future of the world hurrying to its ruin and the power of prayer to change these events. Mirjana receives an understanding of the state of the church with particular intentions and motives for prayer. She is more advanced than the others regarding the revelation of the secrets. She accentuates the threat of punishment.

Marija is responsible in a particular way for messages addressed to pilgrims, to priests, to the Bishop, and to the Pope, to whom she has transmitted two messages: one to encourage his activity in favor of peace, the other to underline the urgency of the threats which weigh on the world.

The youngest of the girls, Ivanka, and the two boys have a much more discreet role, but they partake in the same revelations and share in the communication of messages to the Virgin, whose answers do not encourage the multiplication of such questions: "Why so many questions? The answer is in the Gospel." She has said this more than once, in several ways.

What struck me was the clarity of their gaze. This does not distinguish them in an exceptional way from the rest of the parish. Clarity of gaze is common there, even among those who don't see the apparitions. This struck me during Masses facing the people and in giving Communion. Many of the people there made me think of the parishioner at Ars who explained his prayer to God by saying: "I look at him, and he looks at me."

It was this clarity of gaze which struck me in my conversation with Marija. She is a young girl like any other. She is learning to be a hairdresser. The rough sides of her character (she certainly has them, as anyone does) have been taken hold of, redirected, and transformed by love. I was disarmed by that simplicity. During the conversation which someone had organized for me, I had no more questions. She herself was an answer: "Of everything that you have received, what is the most important?" "The message: reconciliation, prayer, penance. All the secrets force me to pray."

She never mentioned the word "fasting," but I learned that she does not content herself with fasting two days in the week, Wednesday and Friday. She felt the need to add Saturday as a day of less strict fast: she adds a few potatoes to the bread and water. I was relieved because I was afraid that at her age she would be lacking something. Fasting has its own intoxications and traps. But Marija is not intoxicated.

"It seems that fasting does you good. What good?"

"Joy, a total abandonment to God, prayer that is more complete on days of fasting."

"The secrets. Are they going to remain secret as with Bernadette's?"

"No, they have been given to be revealed to everyone."

"What did the apparitions change in you?"

"Everything."

"Are you happier now?"

"I think that we are the happiest people on the earth."

"But before, you were not happy, or less happy?" (Her dimples increased as she smiled)

". . . Less happy."

The charisms of those who have seen the apparitions have developed progressively: apparitions, witness, prayer, joy, and fasting are not a suit to put on; they form a living whole, the organic manifestation of the gift of God. The charisms are simply the gifts of grace for the building up of the community, but first of all for the believer who lives out the charisms. Contrary to an excessively analytical theology, we should not say that the charisms are given for the building-up of the community but not for the person who uses them. If the charisms build the community, this is usually accompanied by an interior upbuilding of the charismatic himself: "He who speaks in tongues edifies himself," St. Paul said in 1 Cor. 14:4. This is a verse too often forgotten in our classical theology. This is what I saw among the young people at Medjugorje. If their witness carries weight, it is because that which they are speaks more loudly than that which they do.

I felt myself outdone, challenged, in my investigator's mindset. I cursed this task (is it a charism?) which obliges me to interrogate, analyze, photograph, pursue into their inner castles these people whose life is so full so that I could obtain the precise details that my historian's conscience demanded. I came to the point of asking myself if archives are not the droppings of life.

The charisms of the young people are becoming more interiorized and reserved. At the first apparitions, they were afraid, they were overwhelmed, sometimes they wept. These displays of emotion have passed. At the same time the apparitions have become shorter. The first apparitions were usually anywhere from 10 to 15 minutes. The longest lasted about 40 minutes. Those which I witnessed lasted about two minutes.

The very charism of being able to see the apparition is destined to pass away. It has already for Mirjana Dragicević. She was ahead of the others in regard to the revelation of the secrets. She received the last one on December 25, 1982; then the apparitions ended for her. The Blessed Virgin thus invited her to return to living by faith alone. At that point she felt interiorly empty, beset with depression, but she fought courageously. She earnestly prayed to see Our Lady again, but subordinated this consuming desire to the wishes of the Virgin

Mary. At the end of ten days she had readjusted herself to the same drab and rocky soil as the peasants with whom she prayed for 18 months.

Mirjana thus points out the way for the others, showing them what will be soon their normal state of faith in the night.

A New Generation of Charisms

At the same time one can see the first process of transmitting the charisms. It is as though a whole new generation of spiritual gifts, more interior and reserved, is being developed to prepare for what follows.

In the spring of 1982 a prayer group spontaneously began among the young boys. Despite the long time of prayer constituted by the daily celebration in the church, 5:20 p.m. until about 7:00 p.m.—Rosary followed by Mass—they meet again at about 9:00 p.m. every Tuesday for prayer. The priests did not find out about this undertaking until it had been going on for some time. The prayer group was constituted on June 24, 1982, the anniversary of the first apparition. It manifests genuinely spiritual qualities.

Two young girls, each about 11 have been given a charism similar to that of those who see the apparition, but their gift is more interior. They are Helena Vasilj, 11 years old, born May 14, 1972, and Marijana Vasilj (same name but no relation), also 11 years old, born October 5, 1972. These two girls do not see the Blessed Virgin, but they perceive her "in their heart." This is a source of light and contact for themselves and for others. This new charism makes one think of the evolution in the life of Catherine Labouré. After a short period of apparitions at La Rue du Bac (all in the year 1830) the Virgin Mary said to her: "You will not see me any more, but you will hear me in your prayers."

This same evolution seems to be taking place at Medjugorje as well, but in the context of a community, where the new gifts are given to others. These latter are quite distinct from their predecessors. Helena has not become part of the group who see the apparitions. Involved as they are in this movement of grace where messages play a role, she felt the desire to know the secrets and the final sign whose date is known by the other young people, but her prayer to Our Lady received this response: "Excuse me! That gift is for the others; it isn't yours. What the six young people have said will happen. It is for you to believe it like the rest." The Virgin herself kept Helena's charism in its own sphere. When difficulties arise, she says to Helena: "Do not defend yourself, but rather pray."

Helena does not try to play any role. When anyone consults her, she sometimes answers in the name of Our Lady, from whom she looks for light: "Why ask so many questions? Everything is written in the Gospel." Or again: "Read the Gospel and you will understand everything."

I asked her: "What does the Virgin want? What is her message?" She recollected herself with her hands in front of her blue eyes. She was seated on the very ordinary sofa in her modest home. She had on a sweater and blue jeans. At the end of her prayer she only said: "Peace. It is for this that the Holy Spirit came down on earth." The urgency of the message was discussed: "Don't get agitated about this. Understand well that peace has to come from us. We have to build peace in ourselves, then others will believe us. Let's put our own hearts at peace." I asked her what was a trick question, considering the tensions preoccupying everybody that had come up with the Bishop: "I'm going tomorrow to see the Bishop. Do you have anything to tell me from the Virgin?"

She recollected herself again: "Nothing to say. Our Lady desires peace."

Amid the difficulties which are not lacking, the words of wisdom which she receives go beyond her capacities as a child even though they retain a certain simplicity: "Pray. Be joyful and in peace. When God begins a work, no one can stop it."

I asked her a question about ecumenism, which had been the content of a message that had been commented upon. She did not understand the word and returned to the most essential thing, what Our Lady is asking: "Today, before anything else, prepare your hearts because Jesus is born tomorrow (it was Christmas Eve). Pray, pray, and everything will be clear."

I felt awkward and outdone by this simple little girl, so intelligent, for whom everything begins with a deep interior life. Her concentration is never tense. Her words have nothing solemn or oracular about them. She has the tone of a child of her age and the relaxed style of her generation. She does not force any words and does everything with poise, with a healthy balance of body and spirit. When I wanted to photograph her on the next day, it was as though she withered before the lens. Her eyelashes closed over her blue eyes, her head leaned slightly forward, she was open, gracious and modest, but there was no one there. She waited with perfect patience until it was over. I asked the priest who is closest to her to talk with her so that some human contact would give her life again (see below, p. 99).

It was on December 15, 1982, that she received the gift of this interior light . . . ten days before Mirjana stopped seeing the apparition. A mysterious transition.

Helena has no airs of a mystic, even to a certain degree. On Christmas Day I could clearly see her during the whole Mass because she was in the first pew with the other children in front of the creche built into the altar. She was praying (prayer in her case is a permanent state) but with the distractions of a child. She was aware of everything. She turned her head to look behind her, she had a brief contact and exchanged a smile with the girl at her side during some moments of the long ceremony. She looked after her brother, a little blonde of about 2 or 3 years, for whom the ceremony was even longer. He had a little box which, it seemed to me, had cough drops in it. It had a metal top and was hard to open. Helena diligently invested her time and persevered until she opened it. This brought a charming smile; her little brother was happy too, but like a child for whom everything that happens is due to him. He disappeared, seated on the kneeler in front of the creche. She gently caressed his hair, which you could just see. She took him up in her arms. It was a perfectly maternal instinct, relaxed, happy, with an easy smile. Prayer and mysticism do not take one from the basic realities. The intensity of her prayer did not diminish her openness to everything else.

These are but some of the branches on the living tree at Medjugorje. I am far from describing everything.

The Words Of The Virgin Mary

A book about Medjugorje ought to present some words pronounced by the Virgin and heard by the young people. For them it is, along with the apparition itself, the most important thing, and it is the part of the message that can be communicated.

This is not an easy task. There are a great number of words, and they have not been kept methodically. The first register of the parish, where the events had been written, has been confiscated. Many of the words have been repeated without anyone making an attempt to write them down.

This lack of completeness is not unique. In the Gospels we only have a selection of the words of Christ, and they are not dated. At Lourdes, as well, for years people cared little about chronology. Bernadette lumped all the words of the Virgin together, dating them to February 18. It required considerable work to restore each to its proper date. At this stage of the earliest information about Medjugorje, it seems to us useful to gather up the significant words with their date before trying to disengage the overall meaning as it appears from the inside to those who are living the message.

This will be but a selection because there have been so many words at Medjugorje. They can be divided into three categories.

Pedagogy And Intimate Conversation

The daily conversations between Our Lady and every member of the group constitutes the largest part of the dialogue. It is an affectionate exchange of primarily personal concerns, as is the conversation of any mother with her child. It is as well a formative training for their faith. It is not for us to enter into this special area; it is most often the personal affair of each one.

The Secrets

We can hardly say anything about the ten secrets which the young people keep to themselves and designate among themselves by their number: one, two, three, etc. We have already seen that Mirjana received the last secret on Christmas Day 1982. This last secret and the next to last speak about punishments for the sins of the world. The young people know the date when these secrets will be divulged. They say that three days afterward a sign will be left on the mountain for those who do not believe. It will be a sign which remains. We know nothing more.

The Words Of The Message

The Virgin insists on the urgency of believing the message: "Many people will not believe you, and many fervent believers will grow cold. But as for you, remain firm and exhort people to urgent prayer, to penance and to conversion. Finally, you will be the happiest." And again: "You must be a sign." We will restrict ourselves here to words that are clearly dated and which concern the *message*.

The first apparition, June 24, at Podbrdo, was silent.

June 25, at 6:30. Mirjana Dragicević asked: "Leave us some signs to convince people. They are saying that we take drugs.

Our Lady did not answer, but she began to pray with the young people seven times the Our Father, the Glory Be to the Father, and the Creed. There is a local tradition of saying seven times the Our Father, Hail Mary, and Glory Be to the Father. The addition of the Creed, I was told, comes from the Virgin. Then she intoned a chant known by the youngsters: "Come, come, Lord!" It is the *maran atha* of St. Paul (1 Cor. 16:22).

The third day, June 26, Our Lady said to the young people, who were afraid that Satan was disguising himself as an angel of light: "I am the Blessed Virgin Mary."

The fourth day, June 27, Mary said to Marija Pavlović: "Peace, peace . . . nothing but peace. Men must be reconciled with God and with one another. For this to happen it is necessary to believe, to pray, to fast, to go to confession." She heard these words after the apparition as she was going down the hill. During the apparition the Virgin held in her hand a large Cross, gray in color, with no corpus on it.

Mary repeated this message many times on the following days. On June 28 or 29, they asked her: "How should we pray?" The Virgin answered: "Continue to recite seven times the Our Father, Hail Mary, Glory Be to the Father, and the Creed.

Vicka Ivanković had learned this prayer from her grandmother (except for the Creed, it seems). Our Lady encouraged the young people to recite it. It was on this day that she began to call them "my angels" or "my children."

Did the initiative for fasting come from the Virgin? It is not certain. It seems to have begun quite early in keeping with the Franciscan tradition of the parish which was brought to life by the apparition. Apparently after having experienced the benefits of the fast they asked the Virgin two months after the first apparition: "What is the best fast?" "A fast of bread and water." Thus they began the custom of fasting on Wednesday and Friday, to which some among them (notably Vicka and Marija) add a fast on Saturday and nine consecutive days of fast before December 8.

At the beginning of July 1981, the young people transmitted this message to priests and religious: "You must believe firmly and watch over the faith of the people."

On August 6 the message of peace was written in the sky as though written by an invisible hand: *Mir* (Peace). This sign was repeated several times. Many witnessed to having seen it. It was at the end of August 1981 during an apparition in the village of Bijakovići that the Blessed Virgin said: "I am the Queen of Peace."

She expressed the desire that June 25, the date of the second apparition (and the first apparition to the six who were to form the definitive group), be celebrated under the title "Queen of Peace." It was a striking coincidence: June 25 is also the anniversary of the last appearance of Our Lady at Marienfried in the parish of Pfaffenhofen near Ulm.

On August 7 she made the young people come up to the mountain about 2:00 in the morning and pray that people would do penance for sinners (this echoes the message of Lourdes). She promised to give a special sign so that the world would believe.

A little later, probably September 4, she specified that the sign would be given when all the apparitions were over. At the end of September she specified the exact time (except to Marija Pavlović) but under the seal of the secret.

In October, 1981, the Blessed Virgin answered two questions posed by the priests of Mostar to Marija: [Regarding Poland] "In a little while there will be great conflicts there, but the just will prevail."

[Concerning the Eastern countries] "Russia is the people where God will be most glorified. The West has advanced civilization, but without God, as though it were its own creator." What she added after this concerning the West seems to pertain to the realm of the secrets.

The Blessed Virgin had already spoken about conversion. On December 7, 1981, the Vigil of the Feast of the Immaculate Conception, she said: "Many people are on the road of conversion, but not all."

This theme will recur frequently. On December 8, 1981, on the Feast of the Immaculate Conception, the youngsters expected to find her full of joy, as on the other feasts, but they saw her on her knees imploring Christ. She said in substance: "My beloved Son, I beg you, pardon the world for the heavy sins by which it offends you."

On July 21, 1982, the six heard this phrase: "Prayer and fasting can prevent even war."

On August 6, 1982, the Blessed Virgin recommended monthly confession, and this message was put into practice in the whole parish. At the beginning of each month a triduum was established within the context of the daily liturgy, Friday, Saturday, and Sunday, preceded by adoration of the Blessed Sacrament on Thursday. On the day of confession, 30 confessors are required, and they are busy all day.

In the spring of 1983: "Hasten your conversion. Do not wait for the sign that has been announced. For the non-believers it will already be too late for them to have a conversion. You who believe, be converted and deepen your faith."

On April 20, 1983, one of the group saw the Virgin Mary in tears for sinners: "I want to convert them, but they are not converted. Pray, pray for them. Do not wait . . . I have need of your prayer and your penance."

On April 26, 1983 (to one of the group): "The only word which I wish to speak is the conversion of the whole world. I wish to speak it to you so that you can speak it to the whole world. I ask nothing but conversion . . . It is my desire, be converted . . . Leave everything. That comes with conversion. Goodbye now, and may peace be with you."

June and July 1983 were marked by the messages of Helena, which are of a different type than those of the group that sees the apparitions. These messages have the function of putting the message into practice and interiorizing it.

On June 16, 1983, she transmitted this message: "I have come to tell the world: God is truth. He exists. In him is true happiness and abundance of life. I present myself here as the Queen of Peace to tell the world that peace is necessary for the salvation of the world. In God is found true joy from which true peace flows."

June 23, 1983: "Love your enemies. Pray for them and bless them."

Then came some directives for prayer.

June 28: "Pray three hours a day . . . You pray too little. Pray at least half an hour morning and evening. Consecrate five minutes to the Sacred Heart; every family is its image."

These words were preceded by advice of a more ascetic nature (June 16): "Abandon yourself totally to God. Renounce disordered passions. Reject fear, and give yourself. Those who know how to abandon themselves will no longer know either obstacle or fear."

On July 4 the message was addressed to the whole parish, insisting on the spirit of prayer and on its quality: "You have begun to pray three hours, but you look at your watch, preoccupied with your work. Be preoccupied with the one thing necessary, and let yourselves be guided by the Holy Spirit in depth. Then the work will go well. Do not rush. Let yourselves be guided, and you will see that everything will be accomplished well."

At about the same date came another invitation linked to the tensions which were beginning to emanate from the Bishop's house: "Fast twice a week for the intention of the Bishop, who carries a heavy responsibility. If there is need, I will ask for a third day. Pray for the Bishop every day."

July 26: "Be alert. This is a dangerous time for you. The devil will try to turn you from this way. Those who give themselves to God will be the objects of attack."

August 2, 1983: "Consecrate yourselves to the Immaculate Heart. Abandon yourselves totally. I will protect you. I will pray to the Holy Spirit. Pray to him yourselves."

August 15, 1983: "Satan is enraged because of those who fast and are converted." (There are many in the parish who fast twice a week.)

On August 25, on the occasion of a particular problem: "Do not be preoccupied. May peace reunite your hearts. The trouble comes only from Satan."

At the time for returning to school, for those of the group who were going to be back in the secular environment of the schools and cities, came the words: "Be alert not to diminish the spirit of prayer."

October 20, 1983, for the new prayer group of young people: "The Virgin asks for this commitment for four years. This is not yet the moment to choose your vocation. The important thing is to first enter into prayer. Afterwards, you will make the right choice."

The message for the whole parish on the same date: "All the families should consecrate themselves to the Sacred Heart every day. I would be very happy if the whole family were to come together for prayer every morning for a half hour."

October 21: "The important thing is to pray to the Holy Spirit that he descend. When you have him, you have everything. People make a mistake when they turn only to the Saints to ask for something."

Because it was said that the secret implies punishments and catastrophes that cannot be avoided but only alleviated, Helena questioned the Virgin Mary about this dramatic future. She received this response: "This comes from false prophets. They say: 'On such a day at such a time there will be a catastrophe.' I have always said: 'The evil (the punishment) will come if the world is not converted.' Call people to conversion. Everything depends on your conversion."

On December 15, 1983, Helena began to receive instructions concerning faith, which she recorded in writing.

The Meaning of Medjugorje's Message

As these are being written in September, 1984 the apparitions are still going on. However, it is important to give some sort of resumé of the salient points of the message in an ordered form so that these can be appreciated.

The apparitions seemed to be coming to an end at the beginning of 82   1984. They became much shorter, averaging about a minute each.

Does this reduction indicate that the apparitions are just about to end? All of the young people have received nine of the secrets, except Vicka, who has received eight. When they have received ten they will not see the apparitions any longer, as is already the case with Mirjana, who received the last secret at Christmas, 1982. Surprisingly enough, the apparitions have continued throughout the whole of the year in this very shortened form.

The objection that there are simply too many apparitions (more than 1,200 now) is being made once again. This is not, however, a serious objection. During the Middle Ages certain mystics received communications of this type throughout their whole life and this was no obstacle to their credibility or their canonization. The life of the Church, as well as the people of God in the Old Testament, oscillates between periods when the complaint is heard, "there are no prophets in Israel" and periods when visions and prophecies seem to abound almost excessively. Perhaps the seriousness of the period in which we live and the inertia of the world despite the voices from heaven explain this large number of apparitions at Medjugorje. The prolongation of the apparitions has proved very useful as a pedagogical means of deepening the message in the parish and extending it out to the whole world.

This burning message given as a free grace poses a question of conscience. On the one hand, the appeal from Medjugorje has stirred up among many people an increase of faith, prayer and spiritual commitment. Their life has been renewed by this grace which they wish to deepen and spread to others. On the other hand, the Commission of Enquiry began its work on March 25, 1984 under the Presidency of the local Bishop, the "first member of the Commission," asking people not to speak about the apparitions and dissuading pilgrimages to Medjugorje.

We must reconcile these two apparently contradictory directives: that of the Virgin who speaks of the urgency of the times, and this call to wait for an official judgment, which Rome has advised be not made hastily. How can this very judgment be a positive one if the tree which is bearing these fruits is uprooted? This conflict of obligations is not easy to resolve, but certain people have found a solution. For many the grace of conversion and their daily prayer continue in a very discreet and reserved way. They did not call their trip to Medjugorje a "pilgrimage". In acting this way they are in accord with the directives of the Bishop who has made it clear that he has not given a formal command but rather prudent advice. This advice should be listened to and it is. The important thing is that the quality of spiritual life and the fruits that it bears continue to grow.

This very growth which is proceeding at a dizzying pace at Medjugorje could stir up another objection: is it possible to live at such a level? Is there not too much prayer? Is there not a danger that there will be a rebound effect after this excessive intensity? August 5, 1984 was a day of almost uninterrupted prayer which took hold of the village and its 30,000 to 40,000 visitors.

It was not a unique day. This village of peasants lives out a rhythm of prayer of three hours a day. The young people pray much more than that. Ivan and Jakov, for example, very often go at night to pray on the mountain, either by themselves or with prayer groups. When I wanted to speak with the young people just before I left on August 10, I went along with Tomislav Vlašić and we found them at Jakov's house during the usual time for siesta. They were reciting the rosary in a small room with the venetian blinds drawn, despite the fact that they were going to recite the rosary with the parish that night as every night at 6:00. Was not this too much? You could ask that question. I myself would have been uneasy if I had not seen so often the relaxed air of the young people, their spontaneity, their love of play, their good humor and the absence of all feverish intensity. Yes, they stand up well under a critical eye. Their balance is healthy even amid the daily trials that are the lot of every human being. That very day, Vicka had had a terrible toothache. She was not at Jakov's house that day but she was conducting herself quite well.

The young people in the group live out the message totally; totally and simply. They are open and available to what is asked of them but there is no obvious show of will power even if the energy of their whole being is engaged in this reality. Their example commends itself. I do not say this to canonize them or out of some blind enthusiasm. It is a fact. We should thank God for it and pray for them. Their burden is very heavy, and I sometimes ask myself how they carry it so serenely.

One of the difficult questions that I asked Ivanka that day was: "As someone who sees the apparitions what is your most difficult trial?"

She reflected for a moment calmly and then answered with a shrug as if the question did not have much sense. They bear the trial, which is easy for all to see, without realizing it, as good soldiers carry a heavy pack on a forced march without ever thinking of putting it down along the road. Up until my last visit, it had seemed to me that Ivanka, pretty and happy all the time, was the most superficial, of the group. That may have been true up until last year, but it is true no longer. She has deepened considerably because of her daily prayer.

longer. She has deepened considerably because of her daily prayer. For this as well, I can only give thanks without being able to pass along any details. Ivanka, in this regard as well, does not have many answers for analytical questions. Her answer is her openness.

These young people are a grace given to the Church. They support one another in a marvelous way. I am concerned only for Mirjana, who just now is living at Sarajevo and in a hostile atmosphere. Perhaps the witness she bears will always be more tragic, more marked by suffering as it has been up to this point. Perhaps she has a mission to show forth in ordinary life the difficulty of living out faith in the darkness and in solitude. The most obvious witness at the moment is the group of five who come together so spontaneously without any isolation and who understand and support one another without difficulty despite their deep differences. The message is not restricted to words alone, it is more eloquent in the life of the group which I am beginning to get to know.

Let us try now to summarize the message and to reflect on its meaning on both a theoretical and practical level. On the theoretical level, certain readers would like to find here a synthesis of the message. There is nothing artificial about it. It is very simple. In can be expressed in a few words which are cries from heaven calling us back to the very first words of the Gospel: God, faith, conversion, prayer, awareness of the sin in the world which the Tempter knows well how to stir up. One could say that these are very ordinary words; that is true. But these very ordinary truths are the essential things. Let us not forget what is truly essential.

1. An Urgent Message

The words are given a personal quality because of Mary who repeats them with a new tone, and because of the young people who receive them. This is keenly appreciated by the large numbers of people who write to me every day: "I read your book. I am not given to apparitions but I have found once again a life of prayer. God exists and we know that better now. He has not forgotten us. He is waiting for something from us. This is urgent. . . ." The newness of the message and its relevance is found in the urgency of the situation in which our world finds itself.

Ever since the nineteenth century this world has welcomed, as though it is good news, what people call "the death of God." Man, finally free, has become his own god. He can now enter on the way of progress with no inhibitions. According to those who rely completely on science, man is going to be able to resolve by himself all his

85

problems, including the problem of war and even the problem of death. It is thought that there will be a scientific means found to overcome this last final disaster which overtakes every human life. In this triumphalistic spirit the world has calmly given itself over to sin, to the most elemental desires of the human person, which often become the religion and the morality of the world. From this has come the worst of slaveries, the worst of violence and the worst despair.

The conclusion of the Virgin Mary is that this calm abandonment to sin has placed the world in a state of self-destruction, with no faith and no law, and therefore with neither order nor meaning in life, and this is occurring among Christians. In how many so-called Christian countries has the prestige of the human sciences and the cult of the human brought about forgetfulness of God, of his truth and of his grace? In how many Christian milieux has the demand of life given way to the easy path?

Self-destruction because of sin; this is precisely the message of the ten secrets which have not yet been divulged but are destined to be so.

The first possibility of self-destruction that comes to mind is that of an atomic war. After a time of détente during the era of Kennedy and Kruschev, aided by John XXIII, the leaders of the world now can only think of safeguarding peace through the "balance of terror." This is the formula of those who devise world strategy. In each camp we hear it said: "Peace can only be maintained by the arms race. If I am the stronger I can assure peace. If I am not, the other side will destroy me. Therefore, I must always be the stronger." This gives rise to an unbridled escalation which has neither limit nor end, and which has already been able to stock-pile means of destruction which would suffice to annihilate all life on this planet. In her message at Medjugorje, Mary has not insisted much on these obvious facts which are all too clear to everyone.

However, Mary has insisted more on the self-destruction of so many men, so many human communities and families eaten up by the scourge of fear, resentment and misunderstanding. Why do men no longer think of how to preserve love among themselves when it is the foundation of all life and all human happiness? Why is it that this wonderful gift of love so full of hope at the time of marriage is taken so lightly, lived out so poorly and finally wasted? And in the domain of social relationships, certain Christians approve, if not of hate, at least of class struggle and aggression as the solution to problems. We can see here as well other expressions of the balance of terror: threat against threat, extortion against extortion, every man must defend himself. Nonetheless, history shows us that good human relations and true peace are not brought about by violence. We have only to look at a St. Irenaeus or a St. Francis of Assisi, a Ghandi, a Martin Luther King, Jr. or a Mother Teresa. Man is clumsy in conflict.

It might be said that this new dimension to an ancient message, that is the risk of self-destruction which hangs over the world, is a return to fear and to a punishment psychosis. People object to Medjugorje: John XXIII rejected the prophets of doom. He restored a Christian optimism based on hope. Is not Medjugorje a return to fear and to a punishment psychosis? Do not certain of the young people use the word punishment or chastisement?

As a matter of fact, the word punishment is a superficial theme and is used only by some of the group, most notably by Mirjana. The message as she expresses it assumes an eschatological and dramatic form. She says that these are the last apparitions. Does that not mean that this is the end of the world?

Tomislav Vlašić, the spiritual director of the group, asked her about this on January 10, 1983: "What does this phrase mean: 'These are the last apparitions on earth?' Should we understand that these are the last for our times, for this time in the life of the Church, or that there will be no more apparitions on earth?" She answered: "I don't know exactly. The Virgin only told me that these would be the last apparitions on earth. That is how I understood it. I don't know any more."

According to Mirjana herself, the eighth secret (whose import was terrifying, as was that of the ninth and tenth secrets according to her) has already been revoked or lessened through prayer. Helena, about whom we will be speaking later, says that there is no inevitability about the punishment: prayer can accomplish everything.

The threat which humanity has caused to weigh upon itself, is due to the fact that we have given ourselves over to sin. The Virgin Mary responds to this dilemma not by proposing some sort of magical solution but by urging a deep and interior rebuilding of human and Christian life. The young people and the parish of Medjugorje give us an example, and this is spreading widely today.

2. The Key Words Of The Message

Let us take the key words one by one and reflect upon them. They are the first words of the Gospel found in the preaching of John the Baptist.

A. God

The first word is God. The official atheism of the East has tried to eliminate God, and the practical materialism of the West has sometimes done this more thoroughly. God exists, he loves us, but he has created us free and will do nothing for us without us. This is the very law of creation, in fact it is the law of love. This is the way of salvation which respects the reality of man. It is God, revealed in Jesus Christ, become man with us and for us. The Virgin Mary's vocation was to confer upon God dimensions that were proportioned to our human weakness by giving birth to him within the human race and family. It was at our human level, crushed as we are by the weight of the world's sin that Jesus Christ showed us his love, a love that went as far as death. This is the way Mary has so often shown the young people of Medjugorje the sign of the passion along with that of the infancy of Christ.

B. Faith

Faith is our means of access to God who has become a stranger in our world closed in upon itself. Our Lady strongly insists on the need for a living faith, the kind of faith that Jesus required. It is a faith which concentrates on God but which knows the power of God to bring about healing, both interior and exterior, both personal and social.

C. Reconciliation

Another name for some of these healings is reconciliation. This was the dominant theme upon which Paul VI and John Paul II based the Holy Years of 1975 and 1983. Medjugorje has put into practice this theme. However, there is still much to do. Reconciliation is possible. It can be brought about within families that are divided and between social classes which are now engaged in the inevitability of a degrading struggle. We may hope as well for the reconciliation between the Franciscans and the secular clergy of Hercegovina, between the Bishop and the priests of Medjugorje. Still more, we may hope for reconciliation between the Croatians and the Serbians; between those who believe and those who, often in good faith, are fighting for atheism. Hope ought to go that far.

D. Conversion

Conversion is a key word, a powerful one. John the Baptizer called people to conversion and to repentance before Jesus manifested himself by being baptized. Repentance is the abiding call of God. Our meeting with God is accomplished from conversion to conversion according to the meaning of the word itself (as with the Greek word in the Gospel *metanoia*). It means to turn *from* sin, from egocentricity, from the empty desires which keep us in slavery. It also means to turn *to* God alone in love. There is a strong movement in this direction already. On August 5, 1984, all records for conversions at Medjugorje were broken. There were 70 priests hearing confessions. God's pardon was poured out in the inexhaustible grace of the sacrament. It would take too long to give some examples.

At Medjugorje Mary is talking about sin in order to talk about conversion and the happiness of coming to know God.

E. Prayer

Prayer is essential to the message of Medjugorje because it is in prayer that we communicate with God, that our life derives its energy and is shared with God. Without prayer so many lives, so many generous efforts, even those of priests, are dispersed for nothing because they are restricted to human solutions. Prayer brings us back to the very source of our existence—to God himself.

People pray a great deal at Medjugorje and many are adding to their time of prayer. This is because they have discovered a thirst for prayer, and along with this they have found the patience and the asceticism to overcome those habits of sin which suffocate prayer in this world.

Prayer is a personal meeting with God. It takes place in silence and within an ordered life. At the beginning it is often a cry of distress, a *de profundis* from the darkness of sin. If, however, someone is faithful in the struggle for prayer, prayer becomes an integral part of life. It is like a subterranean river continually moving and finding its way. It touches the deepest areas of the human personality and purifies even the unconscious. The aberrant drives of the human person need not be repressed; they are rather reduced to impotence by the power of the cross (see Rom. 6:4). God becomes the abiding source of light in our labor and even in our sleep. When the love of God reaches even to our dreams it is a sign that his action in us is not powerless and that it reaches even to the secret levels of our being. The young people at Medjugorje and the whole parish have been asked to give a half hour to personal prayer every morning and every evening. The time of personal prayer is given over to the Lord; the affairs of this world which have such a grip on us are put aside. When we sacrifice our preoccupations to God and direct our concerns to him we find that all the true values of the world are given back to us a hundred-fold. They are now seen in the will of God, in his light and his power. The time of daily prayer can be divided into four periods which represent the four essential ways we relate to God.

1. Praise, Adoration And Thanksgiving

The first act of prayer is directed to God himself because he is God and because he loves us. How often we forget this. We thank God for all that he has done for us: for the salvation and new life he has given us in his Son, Jesus Christ. Praise and thanksgiving reside in the mind, not in the emotions. They are the work of faith. We thank God as well for all that he wishes to do for us and we know that he will never cease caring for us. We can thank God for the future as well as for the past because the Lord has in store for us blessings that go beyond our small power to imagine.

2. Repentance

We are all beset by habit patterns of sin. God, who loves us, and whom we have praised and thanked sees our state with perfect clarity. Every day we should ask him, "what is there in me that displeases you? What is there that blocks the gift of grace and your love? Take it out of my heart, even if I am attached to it. Bring about in me the capacity to go beyond those false attitudes which remain in me and which block the coming of your kingdom."

3. Listening To The Word Of God

Normally we should receive a personal word of prophecy from the Lord through the Scriptures. We may open the Bible anywhere or we may read it in a more methodical way. The essential thing is that we learn to see and hear what the Lord desires to teach us about himself, about ourselves, about his plan of salvation. All of this comes about by the gift of Jesus Christ who gives us his Holy Spirit (so tragically unknown today). This is how our life gets deeper and we are more and more open to the call of the Beatitudes. This is also the way we come to understand Mary, who is such a splendid model. For her everything was grace, and she was graced with being the Mother of God (see Lk. 1:28-30). It is by an intense interior activity initiated and sustained by the Holy Spirit within us that we learn to abide in the Word of the Lord (see Jn. 8:31).

4. Intercession

Finally, we should pray for others and for the whole world. Intercession derives its power and its meaning from the light of God. At the end of our prayer it is no longer we ourselves who intercede, it is Christ, it is the Holy Spirit who intercede in us; and in a certain way it is Mary as well.

Private prayer is not enough. A community is necessary for a life of prayer. The parish at Medjugorje gives us a wonderful example. Everyone of us should try to find something similar by whatever means are possible. Private prayer prepares us for liturgical prayer, for the prayer of the Church in all its forms. At Medjugorje the traditional prayer of the people has taken on a new meaning: the recitation of seven or three times the Our Father, Hail Mary and Glory Be to the Father, and the Creed, or the rosary.

There are other liturgical ceremonies as well at Medjugorje. For instance, the penitential rites which prepare for confession and the uprooting of sin; the adoration of the Blessed Sacrament every Thursday; and most especially the Mass, that fundamental gathering every day. The Eucharist is the source and summit of all other prayer in which the Lord gives himself fully. It is with him and in him that we are able to say in all the fullness of the expression: Our Father.

F. Fasting

Another aspect of the message of Medjugorje may seem to pertain less to the Gospel: it has to do with fasting. Jesus said that his disciples ought not fast because the bridegroom was with them. He also broke with a formalistic exterior fast made to conform to law. He did well to warn his Church about such dangers.

If the Lord suspended fasting while he was with his disciples it was not to abolish it, but to bring it to perfection. He himself began his public ministry by fasting forty days. Following the teaching of the prophets, he knew well the risks of a purely ritual fast (Am. 5:21; Jer. 14:12). He knew as well the danger of pride (Mt. 6:16). Thus fasting, as it came about in the early Church, was always linked to prayer. Fasting and prayer, rather than the sessions of the planning committee, were the source of the apostolic commissions and the ultimate conversion of the Roman Empire (see Acts 13:2; 14:23; see as well 2 Cor. 6:5; 11:27).

Fasting has almost disappeared in the Church of today. That is because it has been understood so poorly. It has been looked upon as a law rather than a means of life, as a yoke rather than the way to freedom. Most importantly, fasting has nothing to do with being sad or in a mood or venting frustrated desires. It is the disciplining of desires born of the desire for the love of God alone. Fasting is not born of misery, it is a share in the happiness of God which consists not in having but in being.

To the degree that fasting was a law of penance in the negative sense of the word, Christians understood it poorly. They were right in fasting. They were mistaken to consider it a burden or a kind of affliction. When I was young, you often heard phrases like, "When he fasts he is in an abominable mood." But this is to fast poorly. If that is the way you fast, it is better not to fast at all. Jesus said: "When you fast, see to it that you groom your hair and wash your face" (Mt. 6:17).

Fasting is not an exterior law, it is rather an interior state. It means openness, availability, the renunciation of basic satisfaction in order to receive God more deeply. This is infinitely more than we give up.

Let us be clear about this, the fast called for by Our Lady at Medjugorje is not a radical fast. Without a doubt Our Lady knows the dangers of such fasts: a sort of interior "high," pride at being able to eat nothing, the lack of key nutrients. That is the reason why she said the best fast is on bread and water. This of course presupposes that the bread is genuinely healthy. Fruits are allowed but nothing else. This allows people to adjust the fast to their health and it is better for their digestive system, especially if the bread they eat is made of whole grain flour. On the level of our physical health we do not fast in order to make ourselves sick, but to better orient our energy and to refresh our system. We must bear in mind as well that our primary fast is from sin. There are as well many things from which we can fast—hours viewing television for example.

The primary reason for fasting is that it adds intensity to prayer. Fasting gives us more time for prayer and if needed more time for rest. At Medjugorje the women who cook every day appreciate the extra time on fast days.

When we fast we have to get rid of the idea: "I'm hungry." This is a psychological state and unless we take authority over these preoccupations we will never mature through our fasting. It would be better to wait and get rid of our self-preoccupation in prayer. As a matter of fact, this false hunger disappears by itself when you do not pay any attention to it. Real hunger is a deep and rare phenomenon which most of us have never experienced. We know what it is to have an appetite and on this level it is good that fasting transfers our material appetite into a hunger for the essential of life. We can also experience a certain kind of tension if we are travelling or spending a long time in intellectual work when we fast. When we stop we are hungry but if we forget this hunger we will soon discover that it is not serious at all.

These minute psychological considerations are almost humorous. But it is better to say them so that people understand that they should not begin to fast unless they can do it with joy, balance, openness to their neighbor, openness to God—in short, if they know how to deprive themselves in order to be filled by God.

In this spirit, a fast on bread and water (with fruit added if necessary) does not mean filling ourselves with what we are about to eat. Rather one should eat moderately at the usual times for meals. Two or three pieces of bread is enough to maintain the strength you need for daily activity. It is also important to drink one or two quarts of water in order to aid in the elimination of toxins. This is one of the healthy aspects of fasting. Our body and our soul are more closely linked than we realize, and this purification of the body is a sign and a help toward the purification of our spirit which is joined to God in humility. We should carry out our day not in a spirit of nervousness or preoccupation, but rather calmly without hurrying. A doctor, who is aware of these considerations, asked me if it were not better for him to fast on Tuesday rather than Friday because his Tuesday schedule was more balanced.

Fasting is a humble means of joining the body to the spirit. If our prayer is weak this is often because we do not know how to bring our body into our prayer. Fasting is one useful way among others of directing our energy which is so often dispersed. This is one of the secrets of fasting. It is a little springboard, quite useful in our movement toward God and toward others.

It is by that kind of love that sin will be overcome, the world reconciled, and the catastrophes, which the world is preparing for itself, avoided. One of the graces of Our Lady of Medjugorje has been to recall to us these fundamental truths too often forgotten and to bring us to experience their benefits.

The meaning of Medjugorje therefore is very simple. It is a return to the beginning of the Gospel, a return to John the Baptizer, the prophet of repentance, prayer and fasting. The rest will be added including the overcoming of the critical situation in which the world finds itself. The process has already begun at Medjugorje. The young people who have seen the apparitions can witness to it. It is up to us, with the grace of God, to do the rest.

What I Saw At Medjugorje

The chapter as I first wrote it stopped right here. However those who read the manuscript expressed a desire that I say here more exactly what I saw at Medjugorje during my visit at Christmas time, especially regarding the daily ecstasies of the young people.

The youngsters' ecstasies and my contact with them form part of a whole that cannot be put in writing. Every description runs the risk of creating the wrong impression. It could evolve into a purely material description which does not arrive at the most essential dimension, or it could try to express what can't be expressed: the world beyond ours to which the young people have access. Trying to put too much down on paper can result in something false and misleading.

Then, too, the very conditions of the investigation prevented me from being, to the degree that I wanted to be, an observer and participant who entered into the experience from the inside with the essentials of prayer and the light of faith. Before arriving at Medjugorje, I had decided not to take any pictures the first day and to restrict myself to watching and praying. However, one of the priests with whom I shared this intention said to me: "If you have to take pictures, today is the day. It is the only day that you will have five of the young people together. After this you will not have more than three or four."

Then I began to take pictures on December 24 with the idea of stopping on the next day. But the apparition was so short and my flash would not work. This meant I had to go on taking pictures the other days since a book of this kind demands that kind of documentation. I admit, then, that these are the things which limited my observations.

On December 24, a little before 6:00 p.m., as on every day, while the crowd was reciting the last part of the Rosary, the young people went into a room facing the sacristy (on the right as you face the altar). I was there with about ten people.

They prayed out loud along with everyone else. A few moments later (the length of an Our Father) their faces lit up and at the same time, with alacrity and in perfect unison, they knelt down, each in his own way. They looked up, all in the same direction. Their gaze was full of love and satisfaction, but their expression was restrained; their faces were without notable expression though they were relaxed and happy. Only Vicka (the extrovert) blossomed with many smiles and nods of agreement, speaking a great deal, as one could make out from her lips though her words were inaudible. Little Jakov tilted his head a little more than the others because he is much smaller than they. His gaze showed a particular intensity, I was going to say avidity. Marija's gentle smile was transparent. Ivan's face (the most introverted) stayed the same. It is clear, however, that he also was absorbed, filled with what he beheld. Less than two minutes later, their prayer began again out loud. They all began together, and this was all the more striking because they began with the third word of the Our Father: ". . . who art in heaven." No one heard the Virgin, who intoned the prayer. A minute later, when the prayer was over, they got up. The end of the apparition did not leave them either sad or disappointed. They remained joyful and deeply satisfied. They went back into the church and knelt down behind the altar. From there the crowd cannot see them because the altar is raised about ten steps higher than the crowd. However, you could hear their firm and rough voices, devoid of sentimentality. When the Rosary ended, Mass began.

On December 25, Christmas Day, it was the same situation except that only four of the young people were present. The fifth had to leave to return to school. On that day one of the Franciscan Fathers performed some experiments to show me some characteristics of the ecstasy. He pressed on Vicka's arm, and this did not disturb her at all. Her conversation and her smiles continued. Then he picked up little Jakov who in that state seemed to be heavy. Jakov's absorption remained the same; there was no reaction. After the apparition, the priest asked the two youngsters: "Did you feel anything when I disturbed you?" There was surprise and an emphatic "No."

On that day, the youngsters said that the Virgin was not wearing her gray robe but a robe of gold in honor of the feast, as had happened on August 15 and other feast days. She was holding the infant Jesus in her arms, as at the first apparition. This was also an exception.

On December 26 I got up at 5:00 a.m. to go to Split to see Archbishop Franić. As I came out of the hotel at Čitluk, which was not heated, it took me a minute to scrape the frost off the windshield of my car with my fingernails. I left early because I had to be back early in the afternoon in order to clarify some points and to see the young people again.

When I returned, I asked them about their interrogations by the police. They were very discreet. Someone there reminded me that the officer responsible for the investigation had threatened them with a revolver: "Is it true?" I asked them. They confirmed it, smiling.

As the time for leaving drew near and fatigue suppressed the other questions, I asked that one of them send to me, if they could, anything that would be useful for the work begun on Medjugorje. Vicka could not take charge of this because since January 7 the Virgin had begun to tell Vicka her life as she had done for Mary of Agreda, Catherine Emmerich and Marja Valtorca. This is part of Mary's training of Vicka. Little Jakov did not want to take responsibility for this. Ivan agreed to do it.

The apparition was a little longer than the preceding ones but much like them in regard to the flow of events: the consequence of their gaze, the perfect unison they evinced at the beginning and the end. There were only three that day: Vicka, Jakov, and Ivan.

Now it was time for me to return to Dubrovnik, a long drive. I had to get up once again at 5:00 a.m. to catch the plane that did not take off, however, because of the wind. This can happen on the Dalmatian coast.

Because of this, I did not attend the Mass on December 26 which followed the apparition. Tomislav was getting ready to celebrate it. As I went up to him to say goodbye, Ivan approached me. He came to give me his answer. Tomislav translated it for me: "Our Lady is praying for this work. Anyone who undertakes it should do so in prayer. It is there that they will find their inspiration."

Why did I have the sense that Our Lady, invisible to me but present to everyone, had come simply to recall to these simple people simple and valid things that the world forgets? These are the things which alone can snatch the world away from the unhappiness it hides, from the self-destruction which its agitation, materialism, ideology, and megalomania are preparing. Is it foolish to think that this message of long-term happiness which they have understood in prayer and fasting could ever be contagious and saving?

The Strata Of Harmony
The First Stratum

The forthright pastoral activity of Medjugorje is an organic whole. It is possible to distinguish three factors in it which are, as it were, three strata—if I may be permitted a geological term when speaking of something which is in reality a vital unity.

The first stratum is the tradition of prayer in a Christian and peasant atmosphere, better preserved here than elsewhere. It made me think of the traditional people of the Vendée of my childhood. There the consciences are clear and the prayer reflects it. The feast days are celebrated in a way that is alive and involves all the people. At every Christmas Mass they sing a long canticle whose every couplet ends with the name of Mary. Someone whispered to me that it dates from the eighth century. This date is not probable. More likely, as Bishop Franić and some others assured me, it dates from the 14th century. It is sung with a rough and fervent intensity. The annual procession to the concrete cross at the top of Mt. Križevac (600 feet high) draws a fervent crowd which has grown in number since the apparitions. At the last feast, September 11, 1983, there were 100,000 people present. In the church I admired the faces of the peasants, men and women. They were clear and strongly shaped. They were better dressed than the peasants of my childhood. A whole civilization has passed this way. The young people of every background wear their hair in a style that shows professional care. Prayer, however, remains hardy and strong, like the land and the nearby rock which become rougher as one climbs the mountain. This prayer is a foundation, a root. The pastoral activity at Medjugorje has brought to life these fundamental realities which elsewhere have disappeared.

The Second Stratum: The Apparitions

These came gratuitously and forcefully at a time when the pastoral leaders of the parish were in no way looking for any exceptional signs. They resisted, but the power of the charism in this most unexpected of graces was stronger. It was like a springtime which gave new life to old formulas and practices.

The Third Stratum

The charismatic renewal came last. The pastor and assistant pastor, who were there at the beginning, were replaced by those who were in touch with the charismatic renewal. Tomislav Vlašić (who came in August, 1981 when Fr. Jozo was put in prison) was already involved. They wanted to nourish the remarkable charisms which had already begun there spontaneously. They were able to use their own experience, and they brought in others who had the reputation of being experts in this area. That was the reason for the course (which lasted only 36 hours) given by Frs. Émiliano Tardif and Pierre Rancourt and Dr. Philippe Madre. Their visit was interrupted, as we have seen, but it was not without effect. Certain fears were expressed (especially at Rome in September, 1983) concerning the risk of mixing together the gratuitous and unexpected gift of the apparitions with a pastoral practice deriving from the charismatic renewal which itself awakens and nourishes the charisms. It was felt that the interaction of these two spiritualities, both quite authentic, would create problems. It might produce a hybrid symbiosis. Another risk would be the cumulative effect of combining the groundswell of the apparitions with an approach designed to awaken the charisms. Would not this combination produce excesses? No doubt precautions must be taken against such a thing happening if the apparitions go on for a long time, but it is more likely that they will soon cease. Then the problem will be the austere return to the usual life of faith. The experience of the charismatic renewal can be of help here, facilitating the transition from exceptional charisms to those which are more ordinary and daily. For the charisms are not dramatic exceptions. They are, rather, humble gifts for the upbuilding of the Christian community.

For the moment, it seems to me that these three strata go well together. They are not three heterogeneous levels. They have harmoniously developed an organic and living unity. Apparitions easily find their place within the piety of the people, at Guadalupe as at Lourdes. I have seen as well in Ireland that the charismatic renewal is able to awaken many hidden resources of this same popular piety. This mutual coherence and harmony augur well for the future.

Whatever may be the discussions and special problems to be considered, the important thing is that this life force be maintained and directed.

Vicka with her family.

Jakov with his Aunt (Marija's mother).

Helena does not see the visions; she receives messages in prayer.

Ivan Dragicević and his mother, Zlata.

Tomislav Vlašić and Vicka

The crowds at Medjugorje.

Chapter
Four

Are The Apparitions Authentic?

Evaluation And Discernment

Mary produced with the Holy Spirit the greatest reality that ever was or ever will be: a God-man. As a consequence she will bring about the greatest realities of the last days: the formation and education of the great Saints who will come at the end of the world.

St. Grignion de Montfort,
(On True Devotion to the Blessed Virgin Mary, No. 35)

WHILE AWAITING THE JUDGMENT OF THE CHURCH WHICH WE wish in no way to anticipate, some evaluation is required in order to measure the possibility that the apparitions at Medjugorje are authentic. These reflections do not intend to short circuit the work of the local bishop, who is officially responsible for this difficult judgment, but rather to aid it. According to the tradition of the church, the extraordinary visible manifestations of the supernatural are an exception to the usual life of faith whose description was given by Jesus when he said: "Blessed are those who have not seen and yet have believed" (Jn. 20:29). As the Letter to the Hebrews puts it, faith is knowledge of things invisible (Heb. 11:1).

When invisible realities become visible, it is neither the beatific vision nor absolute knowledge. It is rather a limited communication in sign, made for reasons of teaching, addressed to a particular time, place and audience. Those who receive this communication are not, for all that, removed from their earthly situation and their subjectivity. Therefore, these phenomena lie along a frontier which makes them difficult to judge. The Church exercises a double prudence.

First, it exercises a critical caution in regard to exceptional phenomena. Ecclesiastical authority applies itself to examining the "pro" and the "con." It must not confuse what is divine with what is human, and it must assess the ambiguity and relativity of these special communications. Second, even where the local bishop passes a favorable judgment, the Church never imposes this judgment under the obedience of faith. The authority of the magisterium demands an unreserved assent to the dogmas of faith guaranteed by the authority of God himself. But in regard to apparitions, the Church attests only to the probability. It limits itself to saying, "There are serious reasons for believing this. It is a good thing to believe in this because these apparitions are producing good fruit," and so on.

The future Benedict XIV in his study on *The Beatification and Canonization of the Servants of God* speaks of the ecclesiastical approbation accorded to private revelations: "It should be understood that this approbation is nothing else than a permission to make these revelations known for the instruction and profit of the faithful. However, the assent of Catholic faith ought not and indeed cannot be accorded to these revelations even when they have been thus approved. The assent of human faith is owed to them in keeping with the norms of prudence when these indicate that such revelations are probable and religiously credible" (II, 32, 11).

A few lines later he added, quoting John Gerson: "Either a positive or a negative position may be adopted, with the piety of faith, regarding such things, provided, of course, that it be done in a manner which does not show obstinacy."

In other words, no Christian is obliged to believe in the apparitions of Lourdes or Fatima, to which both bishops and popes have nevertheless given the highest approbation and guarantee. Rather it would be classified as rash or dangerous to deviate from this authoritative judgment.

Pius X said in the encyclical *Pascendi*:

> In passing judgment on pious traditions be it always borne in mind that in this matter the Church uses the greatest prudence . . . and even then she does not guarantee the truth of the fact narrated; she simply does not forbid belief in things for which human arguments are not wanting.
>
> (No. 55).

Those who have received this grace and its benefits do not have any doubts. For them it is a gift from heaven. They receive it as obviously being a gift from God. They desire to share it. I have experienced this sharing along with them.

However, I also saw the Bishop of Mostar, Bishop Žanić, who is responsible for making the judgment in this matter. He repeated to me with insistence what he had written. There are reasons against the authenticity of the apparitions: statements which have not been proved, healings which have been denied. Everyone should thus avoid undue haste and irresponsible propaganda. "If the final judgment by the local ecclesiastical authority should ultimately be negative, what will the faithful say to those who hid arguments contrary to their position while making unrestrained propaganda in favor of the apparitions?"

The Bishop then added: "These reservations in no way signify a definitive judgment on the part of the competent ecclesiastical authority concerning the events at Medjugorje. But since those in favor of the apparitions consider themselves to have the right to believe them, it is equally permitted to manifest doubts and to prove the contrary, especially if one has reasons to foresee and to fear an injury to the faith."

The Bishop gave these texts to me and commented upon them when I visited with him at 7:00 p.m. on Christmas Day. We had a conversation which lasted about two hours. These texts correspond well to my own intentions. He said to me: "Do not anticipate the judgment of the Church. Seek out the truth, evaluating the reasons for and against."

This was already my plan in the first draft of the conclusion here presented. I composed it before leaving Yugoslavia. What then are the arguments for and against? What should we think?

The Arguments Against

The objections which have been raised or could occur to someone are the following:

Are There Too Many Apparitions?

The objection runs: there are too many apparitions. They have been occurring daily, infallibly, it seems, for more than a thousand days. Is not this a sign that they are due not to a free grace but rather to some human mechanism found within the subjectivity or collectivity of the youngsters themselves?

It is true that it is a good indication of authenticity when apparitions are rare and limited in time. It is a good sign of authenticity, for example, that those who beheld the apparition at Pontmain saw but one apparition (January 17, 1871). Bernadette had but 18 apparitions which lasted from a quarter of an hour to slightly less than an hour. The first 17 apparitions were irregularly spaced over a period of at least two months. The last apparition, which had the character of a discreet and silent goodbye, took place on July 16, three months later. This also is a good sign of authenticity.

But should we forbid heaven to have prolonged contacts? Perhaps there is a reason for this prolonging. The following comes to mind.

We are in a repetitive world. There is television every day. What is not repeated is submerged. This renders the prolonged repetition of the message quite useful.

The difficult situation in the countries of the East, the long organized ascendancy of atheism demand, as well, that there be help and teaching which are prolonged. A long period may be necessary to soften up a world which is little receptive to a message of peace coming from an Eastern country where communication is shackled.

What is more, the great number of apparitions is offset by their exceptional brevity. Having heard that the apparitions lasted 10 or 15 minutes, I was surprised that the apparitions of December 24-26 lasted hardly two minutes.

The occurrence of these apparitions is not infallible. There have been five days when there were none. After the first day, two of those who first saw the apparitions did not see them any longer. For Mirjana, who was particularly blessed, the apparitions stopped on December 25, 1982.

This is not the place to treat of the diversity of the apparitions as well. It will be worthwhile to discuss this when the apparitions have ceased.

The development of the apparitions and certain surprises connected with them manifest their gratuitous quality. They change place in an unexpected way according to events. When the police prevented access to the hill (July 11, 1981), they took place in the homes of the young people, in the homes of neighbors, in the church, or elsewhere, collectively and individually. On certain days one or other of the group saw Our Lady personally, at home. Therefore the group factor is not important. During the apparitions the Virgin speaks sometimes to one, sometimes to another of the young people, sometimes to all of them, in keeping with a rhythm which has its own logic. Each one receives advice or correction concerning his or her own life. When there is a reprimand, only the one concerned hears it. There is a harmonious interplay between the communitarian and individual aspects.

According to the commonly accepted norms of evaluation, these arguments are weighty.

Too Many Words

The Virgin speaks too much at Medjugorje, and that poses a problem, as it did at Garabandal or San Damiano.

It is true that the laconic nature of the apparitions at Lourdes is an argument in their favor. There were a dozen small phrases adapted to the uneducated memory of Bernadette. Then again, there is the silence of the Virgin at Pontmain, where the message was written out silently, letter by letter, being spelled out by the visionaries in the presence of the villagers who posed objections or hypotheses about what was to follow.

Again, here it is possible to find reasons that justify such an exception. Speech that is more frequent and more prolonged may be quite opportune for the church of silence. It may be observed as well that the words of the message, properly so called, that which is addressed to the whole world, are brief and can be summed up in one word: "peace." This explains the word "reconciliation," while the three other words describe the means for procuring this peace and building it from within: prayer, conversion, fasting.

It is understandable that there would also be a more developed exchange between the Virgin and the young people, as between a mother and her children. It is a dialogue where love expresses itself with words that are not important in themselves, but which make the bond human. There is, as well, a whole process of training made up of advice, corrections, and suggestions. This dialogue is prolonged in directives for the community which the Virgin seems so intent upon forming. We ought to distinguish well two categories of messages: those which derive from the young people who see the apparitions and those of the charismatics of the second generation, such as Helena and Marijana, who receive intimate inspirations and messages rather than precise formulas.

The different communications do not have the same importance or nature. They are diversified according to the member of the group who receives them. To what degree should we say that the Virgin adapts herself to each one, as a mother adapts herself to her child when she starts to speak to it in the language of infancy? This is a classic problem when it comes to messages from heaven, even those in the Bible. The Scriptures were not dictated but inspired by God, who enlightened the sacred writer principally on the level of his judgment. Though God undertook the work as principal author of the sacred text, the human author leaves his own personal mark on it. In no way does Isaiah write like Jeremiah, nor does Ezekiel write like Daniel, nor John like Paul. The style, the images, the manner of conceiving of each author leaves its stamp on the work. The laws of the Incarnation, which one can perceive in the Bible, are necessarily characteristic of post-biblical communications as well. These are private revelations in which God does not commit himself to the same degree or with the same authority as he does in the Scriptures.

We have already noted the differences in the messages conveyed by each of the young people. Those of Mirjana have a more apocalyptic character. Is this derived from the message transmitted, or is it rather colored by her own character and manner of receiving?

Basing ourselves on the immense file of Medjugorje, we must one day evaluate the varied character of the communications. In any case, it is not a question of a mere running on with words. As we have come to know them, the words are written out in the coherent simplicity of daily life and in the living movement of a community's ongoing existence.

Are There Contradictions?

But are there not contradictions in these words?

For such a large collection of words, a very attentive study would be necessary. One should not too quickly label as "contradictions" the variations or divergencies between various messages received which have been interpreted (resumed or explained) independently. In similar material, the divergencies are normal and sometimes a good sign of authenticity. The Gospels themselves do not escape this problem. Did Jesus tell his disciples as they left on a mission, "take no staff" (Mt. 10:10; Lk. 9:3) or "take nothing except a staff" (Mk. 6:8)? No one knows. The formulas, materially considered, are contrary, but they signify the same thing: the radical poverty of a missionary.

Concerning the awaited sign which the young people have described, I hit upon an apparent discrepancy. According to Mirjana, the punishment is inevitable. Prayer can but diminish it. But we have heard Helena oppose herself to the somber views of the "prophets of doom" and teach that prayer and conversion can accomplish anything, including the avoidance of this punishment.

107

This is the only point on which I perceived a contradiction in everything that I saw or read. I do not think that it creates a fundamental objection. It merely shows the role that interpretation or personal filtering can play in the message of each one in the group. Is this not the same in every apparition, including those that have been recognized? To what degree do the long secret messages of Fatima, which Lucy put down many years after having received them, reflect her own personal activity? Suppose another of those who beheld the Fatima apparitions had survived and had for his part written down the same message. Would we not have the right to think that he wrote the same thing not literally but merely substantially, with variations which could be discussed at great length? We always meet up with the same factor, which discernment cannot avoid. There is a certain degree of relativity in the message which can be due either to the fact that the heavenly signs are measured to the capacity of the one who beholds them or to the fact that each person has his or her own receptivity and thus subjectivity.

It is not by chance that this difficulty arises in regard to the apocalyptic aspect of the message. This is an area where it is easy to extrapolate. Do the young people tend to think that these apparitions of Mary are the last ones to take place on earth and that that explains their long duration? Will Mirjana tell a priest three days before the first indication in heaven, as she foresees it? Only the events themselves will show if such precision was justified.

The sin of the world, today as in biblical times, deserves punishment. Faith cannot declare the opposite without denying the whole Bible. Nowadays we tend to interpret these punishments no longer as some extrinsic violence administered by the Just Judge but rather as deriving from an immanent justice: sin produces its own punishment. Is this not what we see in the concatenation of wars, violence, and hatred which are daily making the world more unlivable there where both personal and collective sin abound?

If these considerations invite us to moderate the dramatic and apocalyptic traits relating to the punishment, they ought also to give us a more vivid awareness of the grave threat constituted by the combination of evil and the Evil One, sin and the Tempter.

The Phenomena of Light

What should we think of the phenomena of a cosmic nature: lights and signs in the sky over the two hills and in the sun?

This is not the place to enter into detail concerning these things. A complete treatment would demand a considerable critical assessment based upon a collection of data more complete than that in our possession. We will content ourselves with giving in an appendix some witnesses concerning these unusual phenomena which so many people in the village say they have seen (see below, p. 146).

We might ask why God would give a "sign from heaven" when Christ refused to give them to the Pharisees (Mk. 8:11-12; Mt. 12:38-39). Christ was able to refuse this sign to the Pharisees because he preferred to give the sign of healing. This is a more human sign, more indicative of his mercy and his Incarnation. He could have also refused because his adversaries demanded an account and proof of a kind which God does not give. We should think here of our own way of demanding an account from God when it comes to miracles or proofs of the apparitions.

We should thus be reserved in this matter. Should we forbid God to give humble signs by way of light, using a simple symbol preferred in the Bible for the manifestation of God or of Christ? Why would God not express himself in a living language accessible to the poor? Does not the Gospel itself speak of the Transfiguration, and does it not announce signs in the skies for the last times (Mt. 24:29-30 ff.)? Christ did not wish to anticipate these signs during his public life. However, at the birth of Christ, did not the shepherds, endowed with a light in which they recognized the glory of God, have an anticipation of these signs?

At Medjugorje these exceptional signs made a deep impression. They played a determining role at the beginning. They drew the people of the parish to the place of the apparitions. They inspired conversions and confessions. There is no serious objection that can be made in this regard.

On a larger scale, one might ask if there is not at Medjugorje a certain proliferation of the marvelous. However, such things are classic whenever something exceptional happens in the realm of the supernatural. People who for a long time have been closed off to the world beyond have come to experience within themselves the awakening of a new sensitivity which is then perhaps exaggerated. We have analyzed the effervescence when Lourdes began (April 13-July 11, 1858; see R. Laurentin, *Lourdes, documents authentiques*, Lethiellieux, t. 2, pp. 12-29 and 57-86).

It is difficult to give an exact analysis of this period of adaptation to the exceptionally supernatural. To what degree has God disturbed the usual borders of human existence? To what degree have people pushed them back by extrapolation or projection? It is not always easy to determine exactly. Actually, this is the case at Medjugorje given the actual state of our documentation, especially regarding the luminous signs. Were there really such signs during the days which preceded the first apparition, as some say? The cross which crowned the mountain—did it disappear so many times, to be replaced not only by a column of light and the Virgin herself but also by a host of other forms? What should we think about the signs seen in the sun? Have people unduly insisted upon or multiplied the healings, as the Bishop thinks today? Did some of the group (Vicka and Jakov during the fall of 1981) really disappear from the eyes of those who beheld them when the Virgin showed them heaven or hell? Did they reappear after that, coming from elsewhere? Before affirming such extraordinary occurrences, we would need documentation and analyses for which we do not yet have the necessary data. We can only say that this apparent proliferation of the marvelous belongs to the initial period which has been left behind now and, thus, is of but speculative interest. Let us leave the case open without prejudicing its conclusion.

A Subversive Challenge

The Marxist press has presented the apparitions at Medjugorje as a political plot with a religious cover. A cartoon shows the Virgin in the sky, armed with a machine gun, before the visionaries, being urged on by a priest plotter. Medjugorje, it is claimed, will be the reawakening of the *Ustaši*. This was the name of a patriotic Croatian movement which became extremely right wing and violent in opposition to other violence (in 1929 and again in 1941). Cardinal Stepinac and the bishops condemned its excesses. The *Ustaši* have become the bugaboo called up in any situation against any Croatian who defends the rights of man or liberty. The Virgin Mary (whom the Polish newspapers declare subversive today) was not to be spared here either.

Let us leave the calumnies, the quaint and scurrilous polemics. These were launched with impunity even while two Franciscans have been kept in prison since April 1982 for having written articles in favor of the apparitions.

It is clear that the spiritual movement at Medjugorje is purely religious and is obedient to the strict laws of the country which restrict religion to the church. The constant surveillance by the police has found nothing there but the allusions they discovered in the biblical sermon of the first pastor, Fr. Jozo. It is hard to understand in the name of what law the three charismatic preachers were arrested. They came to Medjugorje on the evening of August 23, 1983, and were arrested the next day at 1:00 p.m. for having publicly prayed for the sick in the church at Medjugorje.

But are not the apparitions of the Virgin of themselves subversive in a country whose government is officially atheistic? Do they not disturb the public order? Are they not a good illustration of the principle according to which the Christians of those countries ask for more freedom, pointing to their obedience to the established laws of the country? In this they are but following in the wake of the first Christians, who considered it right to offer obedience to the emperor as to God himself, according to the advice of St. Paul (Rom. 13:1; Tt. 3:1; 1 Pt. 2:13-17).

In fact, the challenge of Medjugorje is taking place within the context of complete obedience to the laws of the country. The parishioners are not armed, as were those of the Vendee. They left the mountain of the apparitions when it was forbidden to them by the police. It was at the request of the young people that the Virgin began the apparitions at their homes and then in the church. For the church building is precisely the place where the Marxist regime considers itself bound to accord religious liberty. It owes this to the liberalism of the 19th century left. The apparitions are not a spectacle. They take place discreetly in the room opposite the sacristy which up to that point had been a storeroom.

If the apparitions must be seen as subversive, as the propaganda suggests, it is the subversion which Christ has always brought. Since the time of the Roman Empire, this kind of subversion has respected the established order, as Paul expressly states. It is the peaceful subversion of the Magnificat which fills the poor and frustrates the powerful (Lk. 1:51-53).

To sum up: the apparitions at Medjugorje maintain a discreet and private atmosphere which is without precedent.

Exaggerations

Is there reason to regret or fear an excessive fervor at Medjugorje? So many hours of prayer, so many days of fasting, is it not too much? Does not such a steep take-off risk a nosedive?

This is the problem of any fervent community. It was a problem for Francis of Assisi. His Gospel radicalism, particularly in regard to lodging and poverty, could not be sustained. Institutionalism brought it back to something more moderate. Grignion de Montfort, the Curé of Ars, Charles de Foucauld (none of whose disciples could

111

follow his austere life) all pose the same problem. I was uneasy when I saw the level of fervor attained by certain of the charismatic communities, including the Lion of Judah. In regard to this last, and in regard to many others, I have been happily reassured because the demands of beginning a community were met by establishing a solid base, assuring a sound formation, and avoiding rash presumption. At Medjugorje the pastoral care, which is demanding and austere, has the same qualities. There is realism, a respect for freedom, an attention to each individual, a psychological sense for human limitation, a thorough formation, and an openness to the corrections of the Holy Spirit.

Intensity is always a risk, but it is a risk worth running. There is no way of developing a spiritual movement of this quality by walking well-worn paths. The daily attention paid not only to the Virgin and her messages but also to the authenticity of human relationships, is of such a nature as to facilitate the difficult transition which will take place when the apparitions cease.

The objection can be raised from another angle. The Virgin has insistently demanded that people believe in the apparitions: "Let those who do not see believe as though they did see" (June 26). "The [Franciscan] friars should firmly believe" (June 26).

"Let them believe as though they had seen" (June 28, addressed to the pilgrims).

"Let them believe firmly, and he will be healed" (to the parents of little Daniel, June 29).

"Believe firmly and watch over the faith of your people" (beginning of July, to priests).

Is it necessary to demand faith in this way in regard to apparitions or miracles which do not pertain to the articles of faith? Does this not go contrary to the advice of the local episcopal authority to weigh both the pro's and the con's, to avoid credulity, naive enthusiasm, and propaganda?

This apparent opposition is due to the exercise of two complementary functions in the Church. There is faith, a living and daring movement inspired by the Holy Spirit; and there is the exercise of critical judgment and discernment.

The call to a faith which is quick to seize on the light of God and the hope which he stirs up is essential according to the Gospel itself. Christ required this responsiveness. The faith which he recommends is presented in the Gospels as a hope and concrete expectation for healing, and for God's protection, which is able to transform personal and social existence. The role of prophecy in the Church is to stir up this living faith, and the apparitions have a prophetic function.

Tensions with Authority

The most serious objection would be the opposition of the Bishop to these apparitions. This objection circulates in the following form even at the highest levels where I often heard: "The Virgin of Medjugorje blamed the Bishop and sided with those opposed to him and who had been duly punished. An apparition which speaks against the Bishop and threatens the good order for which he is responsible cannot be an apparition of the Virgin; it is nothing more than the expression of partisan sentiments."

Let us try to locate the background of the situation. It reflects one of the most complex situations in the Church of Croatia. The people of Croatia had been confided to the care of the Franciscans up until 1881. The Franciscans took to themselves the resistance of the Christians during four centuries of Turkish persecution which extended to martyrdom. This was during the years 1478-1878. They thus acquired great prestige in the eyes of the people based upon deep ties. After that, in 1881, Leo XIII established the hierarchy of the secular clergy. This return to a normal situation required the transfer of a certain number of Franciscan parishes to the secular priests. The transfer has been going apace during these last 20 years because of the increase of vocations to the secular priesthood. It has produced particularly difficult tensions in the Diocese of Mostar.

In building his cathedral at Mostar, Bishop Žanić, in agreement with the Franciscan authorities, recovered for the diocesan clergy three quarters of that city, which up to then had been confided solely to the Franciscans. There were difficulties because the faithful are attached to the Franciscans. Sometimes this went as far as refusing to accept the secular priests or even walling up the church to prevent their entry. In the conflicts at Mostar, two young Franciscans were pushed into prominence and openly manifested an opposition which among the other Franciscans remained prudent and clandestine. These two Franciscans were Frs. Ivica Vego and Ivan Prusina. The Bishop suspended them and reported their opposition to the Minister General of the Franciscan Order, who dismissed them from the Order.

The two Franciscans, who considered it an obligation in conscience to remain at Mostar near the people they had been serving, went to pray at Medjugorje. They consulted one of the group, Vicka, and received consoling words from her. These reached the Bishop by way of Fr. Radogost Grafenauer, S.J., of Ljubljana, one of the Bishop's advisors. The Bishop collected these texts and made them known in order to alert people to this new and subversive turn of events. This could tend to have people moderate their enthusiasm for Medjugorje and even doubt the authenticity of the apparitions. In the material distributed, the eight texts are presented as having been taken from a "diary" kept by Vicka dated December 19, 1981; January 3, 11, and 20, 1982; April 6 and 26, 1982; the end of August, and September 29, 1982. The general sense of all these texts is the following: the two Franciscans are not guilty. The Bishop does not like them and was too severe. The reason for the trouble lies in the action taken by the Bishop. The Franciscans may remain at Mostar (they had been told to leave). People should pray for them. This whole affair is extremely complicated at many levels.

Father Radogost Grafenauer, S.J., who was opposed to the apparitions, was invited to the Bishop's house at Mostar in January 1983 in order to study "this matter of the Franciscans and their relationship to the apparitions." He changed his mind when he went to Medjugorje. It was in the enthusiasm of what he discovered there that he brought to the Bishop the messages which "the Virgin had addressed to him." This brought about a rupture between the Bishop and Fr. Grafenauer and between the Bishop and Medjugorje. This is understandable from the viewpoint of a Bishop who takes his responsibility very seriously.

How should we evaluate the messages and understand their significance?

The Bishop is convinced that Fr. Grafenauer took the messages from a "diary" belonging to Vicka. But Fr. Grafenauer has said and repeated to all those who have asked him: "Let me say once again, I never saw a diary. I saw only five sheets of paper; four were written by Vicka and one by Mirjana. The four written by Vicka were mimeographed by the two Franciscans (who had been suspended by the Bishop)."

There is still a heavy atmosphere of misunderstanding on this point. The Bishop has very often asked the Franciscans at Medjugorje to give him the diary in which he thinks the messages critical of him are to be found. He came to request the diary on February 9, 1983. He requested it once again in official letters dated April 12 and May 16, 1983 (the latter was followed by a letter addressed to Vicka on May 17). On October 3, 1983 he summoned Fr. Tomislav Pervan, the pastor of Medjugorje, and on November 16 he went once again to Medjugorje with the same purpose of obtaining the diary. Fr.

Tomislav Vlašić reiterated that there was no diary. When the Bishop did not believe him, Tomislav took an oath on the cross. From then on the Bishop has considered him a liar and a perjurer. The whole scene was repeated on December 14, 1983. Since it was impossible to produce the alleged diary, Fr. Tomislav once again asked three of the young people, Ivan, Jakov and Marija, as well as Helena, the question which never should have been asked. These young people are in no way qualified to transmit messages to their Bishop concerning his conduct in such a matter. They confirmed the message but with some nuances. However, the polarization over this question continues to intensify. The response of the Franciscan Fathers to the Bishop grants the fact that the messages relative to the Bishop constitute the principal point to be resolved so that there may be understanding and acceptance of the apparitions at Medjugorje.

This is, however, the first illusion that should be dissipated. The tensions between the Franciscans and the Bishop and the authenticity of the apparitions are two distinct matters. Confusing them is both artificial and unfortunate. It is most important that by all means this confusion cease. This pseudo-essential question should take its rightful marginal place and the two problems which are quite different must be resolved each in its own way.

Were this distinction to be made, the fear that weighs on both sides would diminish. This could only benefit a pastoral activity which requires a humble and mutual understanding between the Bishop and the priests who are faced with such a demanding ministry at Medjugorje.

Regarding the diary of Vicka the problem is quite simple. She wrote four diaries but in none of them is there anything contrary to the Bishop. These are the four diaries of Vicka.

1. The pocket notebook of July 1981.
2. The diary kept from October 12 to December 13, 1981 (a half page each day).
3. A notebook given by Fr. Y. Buballo to Vicka during his inquiry so that she could note each apparition.
4. Three large notebooks. Vicka writes in them the life of the Virgin as Mary has been telling it to her every day since the end of 1983.

None of these documents speaks about the Bishop. The last mentioned above is still secret and Vicka will not divulge its contents until she has received permission from Our Lady.

Nevertheless, it is true that Vicka has said things that are favorable to the two young Franciscans with whom she shared frequently. This provided a motive for the Bishop's uneasiness and over-reaction.

It is very difficult to evaluate Vicka's messages. The way that they were transmitted has always had a negative effect on the situation, both because the Franciscans mimeographed them and because the Bishop tends to use them to prove that they cannot be from the Virgin Mary. Father Grafenauer in a letter of February 4, 1984 has said that the words pronounced by Vicka in this regard are "certainly not word for word from our Lady."

The very environment in which the messages were first collected also leads us to accord to them only a relative significance.

First, the compassion felt by the young people for the two Franciscans who were in difficulty would incline them to respond in a way which was favorable. The whole conflict at many levels seems to have been able to obscure the focus both of the reception of the message and its transmission.

Second, in the history of the Church there are instances where the influence of highly emotional debates has been reflected in the oracles of the mystics even among the canonized saints. St. Catherine of Siena, for instance, believed that she heard the Virgin Mary tell her that she was not immaculately conceived (Benedict XIV in his work on the *Beatification and Canonization of the Servants of God*, III, 53, and A. Poulain, *Graces d'oraison*, pp. 355-356 both discuss this case.)

As Father R. Garrigou-Lagrange said, God permits these failures so that we will make a clear distinction between private revelations and the revelation in Scripture which alone is absolute and infallible. It was in reference to this well known chapter of mystical theology that Bishop Franić said to Bishop Žanić concerning the words to the Franciscans: "The facts should be established more exactly. Even if it were established that the oracles contain an invitation to be disobedient (which would not be attributed to the Virgin Mary), still such a grave error would not necesarily affect the substance of the message of Medjugorje." (Conversation taped and then published in *Sabato*, September 10-23, 1983, by A. Farina, pp. 16-17.)

This troublesome episode, maintained in existence by what are obviously temptations, tends to grow like a cancer on Medjugorje. It should stop. It is a bad thing for the Bishop, for the Franciscans, and for Our Lady herself. Her message is one of reconciliation. In the village of Medjugorje and beyond this, reconciliation has not been an empty word. However, Medjugorje will not be credible so long as the apparitions have not brought the Bishop and the Franciscans to a reconciliation.

We have said that every conflict between episcopal authority and an authentic charismatic movement does harm to both. In these tensions between official authority and the "charisms" which claim a direct line to heaven, the charismatic movement is a clay jar hitting against an iron pot. If they begin to fight in the name of the light they have received, they very often radicalize their position, narrow their horizon, and do damage to their real worth. Throughout history the failure of charismatic movements has not always been due to the fact that they were wrong from the beginning. Often conflict has either deflected or perverted them. In such cases authority is deprived of the living energy of such movements, and the movements, deprived of the help and necessary control of authority, become degraded and deviant.

There is only one Christian solution to such conflicts, as history proves. Each one must forget his own wounds and go out to the other in love without any other motive but to serve God's work. When anything else happens, authority narrows into authoritarianism and can be sterile, and the charismatic community exalts itself for nothing.

Perhaps both these tendencies are manifested in an extreme degree in the case of Savonarola. Alexander VI (not an edifying Pope) got rid of Savonarola by having him burned at the stake, something which neither the Gospel nor simple humanity can approve. But ought we not regret that the fierce zeal of Savonarola and his unsparing struggle for the holiness of the Church could not have found its way into the heart of his adversaries, as Francis of Assisi was able to do for the wolves of Gubbio, both men and beasts? It is for this reason that Savonarola's canonization, not unreasonably desired by some, will never happen despite the justice of his cause. For him to be canonized it would be necessary to find in him the existence of a humility like that of Joan of Arc, another charismatic burned at the stake and canonized.

In this regard, Grignion de Montfort is an example. He thanked God and he thanked his opponents (often bishops) for the blows they dealt him, shocked as they were by his Gospel radicalism.

In the same way we should consider the humility of Catherine Labouré, wounded by her superior, Sr. Dufès. She did not fight or answer back, but after having been insulted she would go intentionally to ask her superior for a "permission," often when it was hardly needed. She thus re-established a normal relationship and proved both to herself and to the superior that there was between them neither bitterness nor opposition. This cost her something. She was endowed with that peasant pride which knows how to stiffen itself against an adversary; this is sometimes a noble and laudable characteristic. Catherine Labouré went so far in this direction that she chose this superior, who had hurt her so much, to be the confidante of her most intimate secrets. It was this choice that finally melted the heart of Sr. Dufès and rallied her one hundred percent in favor of Catherine's charisms. There is no other solution in the Church but that of perfect love.

It is to be desired that the same manner of acting be adopted at Medjugorje. This will not be easy because wounds and suspicion are paralyzing the dialogue for the moment. The Bishop considers himself affected in what touches upon his function and authority which he must defend. The Franciscans for their part have also been hurt, especially when their sincere answer, made under oath, was not believed.

If the conflict worsens, it could be quite harmful. The Bishop, who acquired a great deal of prestige and popular support when he defended the apparitions against the unjust attacks of the atheists, would lose his credibility and seem to be supporting those who oppose the Church. If one day he condemns the apparitions, the priests who are at the parish now would be arrested, as were their predecessors, along with the group of youngsters. They would automatically acquire the reputation of being confessors for the faith, and the Bishop would appear to be their persecutor. Such a situation would be extremely harmful for the life of the Church and could only cause joy to its adversaries. Things have not come to such a pass yet. However, this poisonous tree which we have just described has been able only too well to hide the forest, or rather the garden, where the fruits are growing at Medjugorje.

That is why we can only hope that this interference, extrinsic to the important events, will pass and a reconciling love will triumph. Is not this the very theme of the apparitions: peace and reconciliation?

A consideration of these problems is unavoidable. I have been asked about them by many people, even the most highly placed. Nevertheless, too much should not be made of them. Let us recall the positive elements in the situation:

1) At first the Bishop was very sensitive to the apparitions. His first reaction was to weep with joy.

2) At the beginning of August 1981 he defended the apparitions with courage and strength against all the calumnies put forward by the party in power.

3) If now he expresses reservations and in conscience wishes to moderate enthusiasm and prepare people against possible disappointment if the succession of events does not justify their beginnings, he carefully says: these objections "in no way indicate a final judgment on the part of the competent ecclesiastical authority."

We should pray for the commission appointed by the Bishop which began its difficult task March 25, 1983. The Holy See advised the commission to "do nothing hastily," as the commission itself reported in its first report. The majority of the experts chosen were among those who were opposed to the apparitions. Some among them, after an examination of the facts, have come to a more favorable position.

Arguments In Favor Of The Apparitions

The reasons which argue in favor of the authenticity of the apparitions at Medjugorje, despite the objections which we have tried to look at honestly, are the following:

Doctrinal Authenticity

There are no doctrinal problems at Medjugorje. The pastoral practice and the life of faith are in conformity with the strictest orthodoxy. The Virgin Mary acts in a way which corresponds to her role as it has been described in the Gospels and understood in tradition even though her familiar way of relating to the children could be surprising.

There is no exclusive concentration on Mary. The daily celebration of the Mass shows that she leads to Christ and to the Eucharist. This movement of prayer is not characterized by an excessive Marian concentration. It is perfectly theocentric as this dialogue between Fr. Tomislav Vlašić and Vicka can show: "Do you experience the Virgin as the one who gives graces or as one who prays to God?" "As someone who prays to God."

Post-Conciliar Style,
Openness And Relevance To Our Times

The Apparitions at Medjugorje do not give the impression of a step backward. Though they have points in common and are in harmony with the apparitions of the last century, they do not share the cultural peculiarities of these latter. They fit in with the pastoral life of the post-conciliar Church.

The Virgin encourages openness and ecumenism. At an undefined date, she said: "We must respect every man in his faith. It is never right to look down on a man because of his convictions. The believers are separated one from another, but God directs all the Christian groups as a king directs his subjects by means of his ministers. Jesus Christ is the sole mediator of salvation. The power of the Holy Spirit is not equally strong in all the churches."

The apparitions are also a bond with the Muslims of the country who come to "the apparitions of Our Lady."

Mary does not act like a possessive mother in regard to the six young people. When they asked her what she wanted them to do with their future, she answered: "I would like you to become priests and nuns, but only if you desire it. You are free; it is for you to choose."

And so it is freely and clearly, in love, without any haste that they are working out this decision. Most of them have decided to enter religious life. Ivan entered the seminary at Dubrovnik in 1981, but he had not been prepared for this type of study and his examination results were disastrous. Also, he seems to have been deeply affected by all the questions asked of him in an atmosphere where reservations reflecting those of the Bishop were stressed. He was, however, able to suffer this situation in silence. He does not speak about it. He still believes in his vocation and is looking for ways to continue his studies in a more favorable atmosphere.

Two of the young people, Ivanka and Mirjana, have not made a decision yet. They are thinking about marriage. This choice, made without any pressure, attests to the freedom of each of them.

Our Lady of Medjugorje leads to Christ. When she was asked which prayer is the best, she answered: "It is the Mass, and you will never be able to exhaust its greatness. That is why you should be there humbly and prepared." At Medjugorje the Virgin leads to the Eucharist. The Rosary and the apparition flow into the Mass. Mary has sometimes appeared showing Christ, in his childhood (the first apparition and Christmas 1983) or in his passion. In showing us Christ she continues to say: "Do whatever he tells you" (Jn. 2:4).

The Absence Of Abnormality In The Ecstasies

The ecstasies show forth traits which, according to the traditional criteria and experience of the Church, are convincing in their authenticity.

They begin with a surprising unison, as we have already noted. Everyone kneels with alacrity at the same moment (as at Beauraing), each one in his own way. The convergence of their gaze is remarkable. Little Jakov looks up. Ivan, the tallest, looks practically straight ahead. The only normal explanation for this is that the object of their gaze has appeared.

Often when they pray they begin the Our Father with the third word: ". . . who art in heaven." The Virgin has said the first two words, "Our Father," and they are not heard. The young people's voices become inaudible simultaneously at the beginning of the ecstasy though they continue to speak in a distinct manner. A deaf person could read Vicka's lips because she articulates in such a precise way. The young people are surprised that no one hears them because they have the impression of "speaking normally." The voices are heard, once again simultaneously, when the ecstasy is over, and five pairs of eyes look up together as they follow the apparition which disappears as it mounts.

The young people's perception of the external world is quite diminished. So their perception of the apparition is preserved from any interference. Dr. Stopar put himself one day between Marija and the apparition. She did not seem bothered. Afterwards he asked her: "Couldn't you see when I was between you and her?" "Oh, yes, but there was something like a mist."

Their reactions are also diminished, but they remain, and that is why Dr. Stopar said that, properly speaking, it is not an ecstasy. Their eyes blink (contrary to what has been said) but less than usual. There is neither lethargy nor feverish excitement. The pulse is slightly accelerated: 85 per minute rather than the usual 60. There is a slight blush. The pupils are dilated. There is nothing cataleptic: no tension, no bending, no rigidity, no bending of the neck backwards. There is none of the hysterical manner which troubles me when I see photos of certain visionaries at Garabandal (though this objection is not decisive in itself, it does indicate a certain accentuation of subjectivity).

There is no emotionally based paroxysm. In the early apparitions both emotion and tension were more obvious. The young people have adapted themselves to this new and surprising phenomenon. Now they are perfectly unsophisticated and natural even during the ecstasies. Their bodies are supple, well positioned and balanced, completely at ease. Each one keeps his or her own character and style, according to different temperaments. Vicka is communicative and talkative. Ivan is calm and silent. Jakov is eager and seems to drink in the apparition with his eyes. Grace does not change nature but awakens it to its diversity and authenticity. The young people are not caught up in any imitation nor formed by the same mystic mold. The ecstasy allows each one, each in his or her own way, to meet with God and the Virgin Mary in a way in which their differences and freedom are not diminished but enhanced to their greatest potential.

But how should we understand the nature of this meeting with Our Lady? Is it a subjective or an objective phenomenon? Is it a vision or an apparition? Such is the classic and tiresome question. I have already noted elsewhere that this dilemma is as naive, as foreign to a correct analysis of the phenomena of apparitions and to an understanding of knowledge in general.

As a matter of fact, when it comes to questions of knowledge no opposition can be established (except in limited and often pathological cases) between what is subjective and objective, as though one had to choose between these two. All knowledge is the act of a subject who attains an object. It, thus, always implies a subjective aspect which indicates the impact of the information, the material means of the knowledge, what reaches the subject, and the personal act of the subject which is the knowledge itself. Knowledge is never the material object known. The subjective is thus the obverse of the objective. It conditions the knowledge act of the subject.

This is true for the most elementary kind of knowledge, that which is considered to be the most objective, the knowledge of material objects. Such knowledge is conditioned by factors of a material order which reach the subject: the vibrations which come from a green tree or a red apple reach my retina. From that point a nerve impulse like electricity is transmitted to my brain which receives and decodes the information. The vibrations which come from the object are not colored. What determines the perception of color is the frequency of the vibrations. The nerve impulses are not colored either. They are physio-chemical changes which transmit the information about color. I know the green tree and the red apple. I see them as green or red because information concerning them is decoded in a coherent way. And by means of this decoding the act of knowledge reaches once again to the green tree or the red apple in a way which is certain. No matter how many people look at them, they would all say the same thing. The knowledge is thus objective even if the colors green and red are in the order of symbol. They cause us to know in a meaningful way the nature of each object. To put it briefly, subjective and objective are *correlative*. Knowledge lies in intentionality, that is, in the objective capacity to have contact with the other precisely as other. But there can be no knowledge without a subjective and complex impact of information on the knowing subject.

There is the same problem when we speak about apparitions. What kind of information brings about knowledge of the person who appears? We do not know since we cannot attain by physical means to the exterior object, as though it were a tree or apple. But that does not mean that the impact is necessarily more subjective than the knowledge of tree or apple which we have just analyzed.

What then is the impact which gives rise to the apparitions? Is it like that produced by the green tree on the eyes of the beholder? If an oculist examines the young people, would he see an image of the Virgin on their retina? I do not think so. One might think of the impact as being produced at a more interior level, be this cerebral or spiritual. In this last case the spiritual impact would normally rely on the mechanisms of the brain which are responsible for vision (or imagination). No experiments have been done in this regard. If they were to be done, they would doubtless allow us to tighten up the way we pose the problem. However, we would come up against a limitation whenever it is a question of knowledge given by a person who is freely communicating himself.

The youngsters who see the apparition are convinced that it is objective knowledge. The Virgin seems to them to be as real as anyone else, with three dimensions, as they say. They can touch her; they have done it.

There is, of course, an enormous objection to their interpretation: if the Virgin were there in a physical and sensible way, as a green tree or red apple, the other people present in the room would see her. But they do not see her.

Should we say: Yes, the Virgin is physically there, but she makes herself invisible to the other people present? But this explanation, according to which the miracle would not be one of apparition but of being invisible to those who do not see, is artificial, if not ridiculous. Knowledge of the apparition is due to an impact too intimate to be controlled or precisely situated. Should we say then that the impact is subjective? Yes, in the sense that every informative impact attains the subject precisely in his subjectivity, as we have already seen in the case of sense knowledge. In one case as in the other, the impact can be the *means* of a genuinely objective knowledge.

That the meeting with the Virgin should have a strong symbolic impact changes nothing of the problem. Even in the order of sense knowledge, green and red are coherent perceptions but of a symbolic order.

In this sense the philosophers of the 18th century were correct when they said that there would be no green or red if there were no subject able to perceive color. These colors have an objectivity, but they require a knowing subject if they are to be perceived as such. Symbolic and real cannot be opposed to one another, nor can subjective and objective. Usually, except for extraordinary cases, they are correlated.

There is an idealistic philosophy which holds that one can only know one's own knowledge. This falsifies the basic evidence which can show that knowledge usually attains its object: we know the other as the other. Knowledge differs in this from physical digestion in which the object assimilated is transformed into the subject. Attaining the other precisely as other is the goal of all knowledge. It is that which defines it and specifies it. We call intentionality the knowing subject's capacity to perceive an exterior object without modification of the subject, which does nothing but know, and without modification of the object which is neither carried into the subject nor exactly reproduced or changed. The object remains the same even when it is known by millions of people as is instanced in a television show.

To put it briefly, the knowledge of sensible things is objective despite the material and subjective means by which they are known. Thus, we know not only the appearance of the objects which surround us but we also know persons whom we love. In fact we know them better. The personal and existential way of knowing is the high point of knowledge. This is the way that the young people can know the Virgin if that person who has left our world to live with God wishes to show herself in an authentic and objective manner. There is no reason to doubt this even if this sensible knowledge is endowed with a modality different from ordinary knowledge. The young people say that they really see her as another person in a way which is tangible, they have touched her (there are studies being done on this point). They perceive her in three dimensions.

That the knowledge of the young people in ecstacy should have a
mode different from ordinary knowledge is obvious. They enter into

another state in which ordinary sensible knowledge is, if not suspended, at least diminished. It is possible to touch the young people, to pick them up, to take flash pictures of them without their reacting in any way. Father Nicolas Dulat, one of the experts in the commission, twice pricked Vicka with a large pin while she was in ecstacy. The video cassette which recorded everything shows that Vicka did not flinch at all. Nevertheless, when the apparition was over you could see that the second prick had drawn blood which left a stain on the left shoulder of her blouse.

On the other hand, this rupture with the external world should not be exaggerated. It has been said that the eyes of the young people do not blink while they are in ecstacy. This is false. They blink less than usual but the movement of their eyelids is observable every day. The young people are perfectly supple and natural during this time, and retain their capacity to react whenever this is called for. A certain suspension of usual sensible knowledge remains during the apparition and seems to be the condition for the perception of the apparition.

Why is this so? It is because the Virgin does not belong anymore to our cosmos. Her glorious body, which dogma declares to have been raised up, belongs no longer to our world of space and time. Her existence is not measured by our time. She lives in God and in God's mode of continual existence. This mode is not measured by succession but is present all at once; it is not progressive, moving through time, it is eternal. It is the same when we speak of space in regard to Mary. She does not exist in our order of space as she does not exist in our order of time. The distance between time and the eternity of God is more complete than any spatial distance. In order for a being, taken up by God to share in his life, to be able to show him or herself in the conditions which mark our history, communication must take on modalities other than those of our world. This is why, from the point of view of the person who receives the communication, ecstasy, that is a suspension of the senses, is necessary.

Looked at in this perspective there is no reason to examine the experience of the young people with suspicion, or to explain their naturalness and simplicity by projecting onto them philosophical schemas according to which whatever pertains to religion is either dream or illusion. The young people speak of their knowledge of the Virgin in a very objective and realistic way even though this knowledge is mysterious and beyond the ordinary.

Knowledge of the risen Christ was of the same mysterious order as the apostles were well aware. He ate and let himself be touched:

these were the most objective of manifestations. Because of this mysterious modality the apostles did not recognize him at once, they even doubted (Mt. 28:17; Mk. 16:14; Lk. 24:26-28; Jn. 20:15; 21:7-12). All of this belongs to the particular manner of communication between the divine (eternal) world to which Christ now belonged and the cosmic world of the apostles.

After listening to what the young people have been constantly saying for two and half years, I have come to the conclusion that not all visions have the objectivity about which they are so insistent. I think that, in regard to the secrets for example, their perceptions and the messages they receive are of a more intimate nature.

The history of apparitions shows that there is a whole spectrum of possibilities.

In regard to Bernadette, I always had the sense that she had an objective knowledge even though her manner of speaking was less clear and less insistent than that of the young people of Medjugorje. In this latter case, some of the communications seem to be of a more intense nature. In my study *Lourdes, histoire authentique* (III, pp. 273-293), I tried to explain how Bernadette's knowledge could be objective even though the numerous witnesses to her ecstacies never saw Our Lady in the hollow of the rock. What I have been able to observe regarding the young people at Medjugorje has convinced me that what I said in my study concerning Bernadette was correct and applies to the young people at Medjugorje as well.

In regard to the ecstacies of Catherine Labouré, a genuine peasant, like the young Croatians today, there were successive stages.

1) The first apparition of Mary seems to have been quite objective: "I made but a step near her, kneeling on the steps of the altar with my hands against the knees of the holy Virgin." Though Catherine does not make much of the tactile sensation, it is legitimate to think that it is implied in her account.

2) In the three following apparitions, the Virgin appeared to Catherine as on the miraculous medal. She said it was like "a tableau" which "turned around" to show the reverse side of the medal. It was, then, not a corporal apparition but an image with two dimensions. The design of the medal implies an artifact, something in the order of a work of art, not the perception of a person in three dimensions.

3) In April 1830 Catherine saw on the wall of the chapel of La Rue du Bac an image of the heart of St. Vincent de Paul:

something full of meaning for her. It was not his physical heart, preserved at Lyons; this had neither the stylized form nor the vivid symbolic colors successively seen by Catherine. Through this two-dimensional image, she perceived what the love of St. Vincent de Paul demanded of her and of her congregation. It was a pure sign of that love which was communicated to her.

4) That is not all. After these very different apparitions, she received this message: "You will see me no longer, but you will hear me in your prayers." I should think that this refers less to something that could be heard with the physical ears than to a communication on the level of the mind, the level of meaning.

Thus, Catherine experienced all of the three classical categories into which spiritual writers have divided communications: apparitions, visions, and messages without any image.

At Medjugorje the charismatics of the second generation, Helena and Marijana, belong essentially to the second two categories: interior vision "by the heart" and an intimate manner of receiving messages. The messages are directed to the personal and communal life of the parish and of those who come to visit: conversion, prayer, fasting, reconciliation, courage in trial. This charism of the second generation can easily continue even when the apparitions have come to an end. It is well known in the charismatic renewal.

The differences which characterize Helena's charism have remained despite her desire to share the experience of the young people who see the apparitions and to know the secrets as they do. She asked this of Our Lady and was refused. All this tends to show an orientation which has its roots in depths beyond us. Neither the young people nor the priests who counsel them, as wise as they are, would have been possessed of a genius sufficient to awaken these complementary charisms which rather surprise them. The priests try only to discern, to help, to give direction, like good gardeners, to the growth of a life which is not due to their resources. They work to secure the best conditions for the development of this life and watch that it does not go astray.

Helena's more interior charism moves in the direction of normal spiritual growth: from the visible to the invisible, from the exterior to the interior. It thus tends by contrast to confirm the objective nature of the apparition seen by the six other young people.

As we try to assess these communications, we are in the position of someone who can hear only one half of a telephone conversation. We can perceive the one receiving the communication but not the one sending it. All the medical tests are in this humble condition. They will never attain to the apparition itself.

We can only observe the state of those who see the apparitions. For instance, the pulse rate, the vascular or respiratory condition are not changed, at least not in the case of Ivan, and they are only slightly changed for the others. The pulse rate goes from 65 to 80 according to Dr. Stopar, who observed them without taking an electrocardiogram. The encephalogram done by Dr. Joyeux on Ivan (May 30, 1984) showed that, during the ecstasy, he stayed in his normal state: neither epilepsy nor dream. This is very important because it excludes the hypothesis of hallucination. However, the object who appears to the young people (the Virgin Mary) will always remain outside scientific experimentation. We will always be limited to hypotheses in that regard.

What we are able to observe brings us beyond two opposing naive judgments: simple imagination and radical criticism.

According to the first of these, the Virgin would come down as though in a spaceship. However, this is absurd because, in that case, everyone present would see her.

A hyper-criticism succeeds no better in accounting for the data when it reduces everything to a subjective state, that is, the creation of the object by the subject. It does not explain either the coherence or the diversity of the phenomena which can be observed. Such a theory covers its ignorance with ideological pretensions which neither prove nor explain anything. As Hamlet said, "There are more things in heaven and earth, Horatio, than are dreamt of in your philosophy." There are more things in communication with God than a rationalist ideology imagines though it put on the air of science, calling up slogans derived from psychology, psychoanalysis, or elsewhere. It does this in order to try to reduce unique phenomena to mere subjectivity by an *a priori* elimination of the possibility of an objective source of the communication.

Briefly, the ecstasy of the young people is a positive argument in favor of the apparitions, one which is being strengthened day by day by convergent medical experiments. This conclusion was already that of Fr. Michael Scanlan, President of the Franciscan University of Steubenville, a man well known for his discernment: "On two occasions I observed the young people during the apparitions. The only explanation which can be given for their behavior is that there is a supernatural phenomenon of a mystical character which absorbs them. Nothing indicates psychic hallucination. The explanation which should be maintained is that there is an apparition of Mary, the Mother of God, who is showing herself to her children, as they claim."

The Normality Of The Young People

The daily life of the young people serves to confirm the analysis of their ecstasies.

At the request of the police, doctors examined the young people. This happened as well to Bernadette at Lourdes. The mission of the doctors was to commit the young people if at all possible to a psychiatric ward. However, they recognized the perfect state of their physical health and most especially of their psychological balance. We should not refuse to recognize that, in this regard, the government knew how to accept the objectivity of a positive diagnosis, one that has been confirmed since then by experts in the most diverse fields. The young people have maintained their calm and their sense of humor amid very trying circumstances. While they were being held by the police, a police officer of Čitluk aimed his revolver at Vicka's chest. She did not budge, but looked him straight in the face. She said to him: "Put your gun away. You know that we are all on economy measures."

What I observed among the young people was a genuine simplicity, neither complicated nor simplistic. Each one has his or her own temperament; they communicate well with one another; some are more aggressive, others look on.

Their attitude is balanced and firm, without any nervousness. We have already quoted the words of Marija Pavlović, who said simply and without any self-exaltation: "We are the happiest people in the world."

This same joy is a sign of health. We would say today that they are at ease with themselves. Their two days of fast (three for Marija) do not change their physical or psychic health but seem to augment it, as was the case of the three young men in the book of Daniel. If their message is serious and sometimes grave, it is never ponderous. At the seminary, Ivan suffered on many accounts. There were difficulties and failures in his academic life. There was doubt and skepticism concerning his experiences. Nevertheless, his teachers recognized that he always remained: "polite, easy to get along with, and devout" (Investigation at the Seminary of Dubrovnik, December 27, 1983).

The easy, natural way the young people behave surprised one of the more straight-laced of the older women, who said to the girls:

"How could the Virgin be appearing to you, when you play with the boys?"

They know how to maintain the right distance between themselves and people who are avid for contact with them. There are no embraces, no exaggerated respect, as grew up around Bernadette, who had to show her annoyance. They discourage these abuses simply by the way they are. The priests who are responsible for them have the same simplicity, that of Franciscans and of a younger generation allergic to anything pretentious. Briefly put, the young people are free beings, even in their relationship with the Virgin Mary.

Experts ask themselves why this is so. They constitute a phenomenon which baffles the ordinary laws of psychology and sociology, as Fr. Slavko Barbarić, quoted earlier, already discovered.

Could the cause be some para-psychic capacity or some other unknown factor? This is uncharted territory, however, which cannot be excluded. But even in this case, we must still try to understand how these hidden natural resources combine with a gift of God that shows itself with such richness and balance.

Satan seems to be excluded because these apparitions lead to Christ, to prayer, conversion, confession, and the Eucharist. If Satan were to work that way against himself we would have to say that he has had a conversion!

The best explanation is, then, that we are dealing with a communication of Mary, the Mother of Christ and the Mother of men. This woman, clothed with the Sun of justice, about whom Rev. 12:1-12, speaks, remains present to the Church. She was the pure beginning of the Church. She was the first to live out all the phases of the life of the Church: the first to receive Christ at the Annunciation, the first to arrive at the fullness of salvation at the Assumption. The best explanation, then, is that Our Lady in the communion of saints is visiting us at this moment when the world is so threatened and the Church is so tried.

An Exemplary Pastoral Approach

The pastoral practice of this parish is likewise a good sign.

The priests responsible for the parish have been reproached for excessive propaganda. I did not find among them anything that resembled publicity or psychological manipulation in order to persuade. The situation in an Eastern country would prohibit them from anything that would resemble formal propaganda. They witness in a simple way to their own conviction, to what they have seen. No one can reproach them for that. Every Christian who lives a spiritual experience of meeting with God knows it to be a good thing and spontaneously desires to share it. This is as it should be. I saw nothing out of order in all of this.

Earlier we traced the development of the pastoral practice in this parish: the two priests who were there in June 1981, not favorable in the least to anything supernatural which was exceptional, vigorously channeled the movement toward faith and the Sacraments. Fr. Tomislav Vlašić, who replaced Fr. Jozo (imprisoned the day after his August 15 sermon) had been involved in the charismatic renewal. He knew how to use his experience of the charisms in the service of a traditional pastoral practice adapted to the people without changing its character. The balance between the charisms and tradition, between the faith and the sacraments, impressed me as being exemplary.

When Fr. Tomislav used the label "charismatic," I envisaged a liturgy of a very enthusiastic style: hands raised, fervent oral prayer, speaking in tongues. But there is none of that at the Masses and ceremonies of the parish at Medjugorje. The liturgy is that of a peasant parish of that country. The quality and intensity of the prayer are demonstrated with an exceptional sobriety.

The Fruits

The fruits of this movement of grace are its best authenticating sign. They are the most persuasive, according to the Gospel, because, as Christ said: "By their fruit you will recognize them" (Mt. 7:16; Lk. 6:44).

The fruits are such that they are most convincing at every level: a human balance, charisms, love. This is true even if it is possible to question whether one or another characteristic is really opportune: human limitations are not eliminated at Medjugorje. The dominant gifts are a naturalness of behavior, clarity, balance and freedom, love, trust in God, and daily prayer.

The most particular aspect of Medjugorje is the fasting. At Medjugorje one witnesses the restoration of a Franciscan tradition, once intensely lived and then neglected. Fr. Jozo Zovko returned to this practice even before he believed in the apparitions. During the very first days, as he asked himself questions about this uncommon phenomenon, he invited the parish to fast for three days.

Fasting fosters seriousness in one's faith and availability for prayer. From Medjugorje the practice of fasting has spread widely throughout the Church to thousands and thousands of people who are experiencing its fruit. The apparition thus comes to the support of the effort of Pope John Paul II, who favored maintaining the practice of fasting in the new code of Canon Law, even when others wanted to suppress it along with abstinence.

It is not a radical fast; it is rather moderate. The young people learned from the apparitions that the best fast consists in bread and water. I gathered from the practice of the parish and from the answers of the young people that fruit is acceptable, though of course there should be no eggs or fish or anything of that sort. Fasting does not make you weak. It is carried out with joy and peace and without any of the anxiousness that can be found in some monasteries. Some people do not understand fasting and thus eat more at the one meal allowed them than they would in an ordinary day of three meals. When you fast well, there is no hunger; you eat a little at the three regular mealtimes. This frees the body of toxins and frees the mind and heart for the gifts of God.

This is the Franciscan tradition, for which fasting derives from the Gospel tradition in which the disciples did not fast so long as the "Bridegroom" (Christ) was with them (Mt. 9:15). The Acts of the Apostles show us that the Christians did indeed begin to fast when the Bridegroom was taken away (see Acts 13:2; 14:23).

I asked Marija: "What does fasting accomplish for you?" She answered me (it was December 24): "Joy, an availability to God, a more total trust in him, and a more vital prayer." In honor of the Virgin, she adds Saturday to the other two fast days—Wednesday and Friday. Saturday is a more moderate fast, however, as she will eat potatoes on this day. In addition she fasts on the vigils of the important feast days; the Assumption and the Immaculate Conception are prepared for by nine days of fasting.

The young people are, as it were, a pilot project. Their example has quickly spread around. In the village, in the majority of families, there is no cooking one or two days in the week. This means more freedom and time for prayer. All of this is happening and deepening without anyone making a show of will power. It is more a question of making sure there is time for prayer without clock watching. It is a means of cultivating a relationship of union with God, and in this there are found strength, joy, and love: the oil that makes the wheels of the church's life turn easily. As is the case with any authentic spiritual movement, the development is from the interior. There is no planning. Faith and what is received in prayer are the soul of this movement. The priests follow it and guide it. It is this power and spontaneity that make such an impression on the numerous visitors from all over the world. I have met at Medjugorje many Americans and even an Australian who made the trip precisely to visit Medjugorje. It was a personal conviction and did not derive from any press notice.

Because this is taking place in a country of Eastern Europe, there is a veritable osmosis taking place between the profound spiritual life of the Church of silence and the churches of the West which are seeking to find themselves.

The development of the whole movement at Medjugorje began with external manifestations and these have deepened into an interior life. The phenomena of light which were the first to draw the crowds are now quite sporadic; now there is the daily asceticism of prayer and fasting.

Healings come as an outgrowth of this spiritual reality. Prayer for healing is always quite discreet, a fact encouraged by the constant vigilance of the government. Thus there is a movement from the visible to the invisible, from the apparitions to formation in faith. Grace and trials of every sort conspire together to the profit of this spiritual life. The pastoral practice of the priests tends to avoid whatever is exceptional, spectacular, or highly emotional.

As we have already seen, one of the young people no longer sees the apparitions. She has begun the route of returning to that obscure faith which will soon be the situation of all the young people: "Our requests are often out of order. We should be asking for the Holy Spirit," one of the young people said.

This reminds us of the words of Christ, who said: "If you, though you are evil, know how to give good gifts to your children, how much more will your Father in heaven give the Holy Spirit to those who ask him!" (Lk. 11:11-13).

This is the experience of every truly Christian community.

A Return to Normalcy

The apparitions at Medjugorje fulfill a function which is proper to them. Before knowing Medjugorje personally, I had drawn up a summary list, as it were, of what functions were fulfilled by apparitions.

- Manifest the hidden presence of God and of those who share his life in glory.
- Communicate prophetic messages.
- Awaken, restore to life, make present faith and especially hope.

133

- Convert people and sustain their fervor.
- Build up Christian communities, stir up enthusiasm and projects amid spiritual inertia.
- Strengthen the lines that connect the communion of Saints.

All of these functions are found at Medjugorje.

Therefore, our judgment is quite positive. The questions and objections, the accidents along the way (like banana peels put on the path by the Evil One) seem to be more than compensated for by the positive fruits which are truly exceptional. What is happening at Medjugorje is at the level of the best of Christian experiences. We see there a very particular grace joined to the charisms which the Council desired to see awakened once again in the Church. This is further joined to the fruits of a beautiful Christian (and Franciscan) tradition. All of this makes for a rare combination full of promise.

Statements Expressing A Favorable Opinion

It seems to me that it will be useful here by way of conclusion to collect some favorable opinions concerning Medjugorje.

1. Scientists

Some doctors have pronounced favorable verdicts regarding certain healings, but it is impossible to use their opinions without creating difficulty for them in their own country. I present those I can.

Dr. Ivan Tole, born at Rodoc near Mostar, who belongs to the International Committee of Lourdes, considers that three or four of the healings are certainly miraculous.

Dr. Ludvik Stopar, neurologist and para-psychologist from Maribor, went twice to Medjugorje and studied the young people according to his own methods which are in the order of hypnosis. He separated the conscious life of the young people from 90% of the unconscious life which supports it. Their account and their answers at the unconscious or automatic level were substantially the same as at the conscious level, where their speech was more hesitant. He excludes the possibility that they could be "mediums." His opinion corresponds to that of the doctors contacted by the police to perform a mental examination and who found the young people normal.

Dr. Philippe Madre confirmed their physical, psychological, and spiritual balance.

Ivan Dugandic drew up a very positive report concerning the young people and the events, which he observed for a week.

Dr. Milan Topalovic, psycho-neurologist and expert in acupuncture, observed the young people during the apparitions. His judgment was also favorable.

Slavko Barbarić, Franciscan psychotherapist and expert in spiritual theology, administered psychological tests to the young people for several months. He is responsible for the study, repeated by Fr. Rupčić, adducing the apparitions as the reason for the coherence of the group.

2. Spiritual Discernment

Many experts in this matter, notably charismatics, have made favorable judgments.

Fr. Robert Faricy, S.J., professor at the Pontifical Gregorian University in Rome, summed up his conclusions in a basic article published in *Feu et Lumiere* (October 1, 1983, pp. 22-27). After having prudently accentuated the fact that "the Church has not yet pronounced itself," his careful examination excludes any simulation or other activity on the part of the devil. He praises "the healthy doctrine, the human and spiritual qualities of the six young people," and "the very positive fruits which constitute the best argument for considering the apparitions as authentic." He concludes: "Medjugorje should be a place not only of national but international pilgrimage."

I collected similar judgments on the part of other experts on the spiritual life.

> **Fr. Michael Scanlan**, president of the University of Steubenville;
>
> **Fr. John Bertolucci** of the same university;
>
> **Fr. Beck** of Milan, Hungarian, born at Zagreb. Today director of a retreat house in Milan. He has visited Medjugorje three times;
>
> **Fr. Thomas Forrest**, who spent two days at Medjugorje.
>
> **Fr. Tomislav Ivancić**, professor of fundamental theology at Zagreb, who also spent two days at Medjugorje.
>
> **Fr. A. Dongo**, Belgian theologian.
>
> **Fr. Radogost Grafenauer, S.J.**, consulted by the Bishop of Mostar because of his prudent and critical outlook, who has become strongly in favor of the apparitions.
>
> **Fr. Hans Urs von Balthasar,** theologian and spiritual author of the highest quality, who has been very interested in

135

Medjugorje. He spoke about it in Rome and helped those responsible for the parish make a positive evaluation of the present and the future.

All these in different degrees exclude a purely natural explanation and, even more, a diabolical influence.

I ask pardon for adding here, without much order, other evaluations collected by Fr. Rupčić, for which I cannot give names, either for reasons of safety or because I cannot make out the writing.

A professor from Dusseldorf: "I have traveled the whole world, and I have never seen people like this. They are alive."

A professor of theology from Zagreb (Ivan Golub?): "I came to Medjugorje and I expected a sermon on Mary. Well, I did not hear any preaching on Mary but rather about Mary, who said: 'Do whatever he tells you' (Jn. 2:24)."

Two others: "At Medjugorje I did not see the face of the Virgin, but I saw her reflection in the face of the people there. I do not know if Our Lady appeared to the young people, but I see that she has appeared to the world." "If Our Lady has not appeared, this receptive atmosphere will make her appear."

3. Beyond Ecumenical Frontiers

David DuPlessis is a Pentecostal leader and a man of great spiritual qualities who opened up the Pentecostal movement to ecumenism and has dedicated himself to a life of extraordinary spiritual discernment. He received a totally positive impression from his visit to Medjugorje: "Despite all my contacts with the Catholic Church, I have never seen such a spirit of prayer. For a long time I have been afraid of your Catholic tradition concerning Mary, because she does not occupy such a place among us. Among you I have come to understand that Mary leads to Christ. I am going to speak about this with the Pope when I see him." This is a good indication that the apparitions of Medjugorje are without any of the historical particularities of Catholicism and thus have a better quality ecumenical dimension.

A Muslim dervish from Blade (near Mostar), experienced in the mystical ways of Sufism, reacted very positively when he assisted at the apparitions in the small room where they take place: "I felt in my heart such energy that I could have cried out. I thought that I would fall into ecstasy myself. I decided to pray the whole night. Do not let people into that little chapel unless they have been alerted. This world is looking for God. If it looks for him, it will find him. If it finds him, it will cling to him lovingly, and he who is in love with God cannot be separated from him by anything." These words of a non-Christian are a surprising echo of what St. Paul says in Rm. 8:35-39: "Who shall separate us from the love of Christ?"

4. How Bishops Have Received The Apparitions

The reception that Bishops have given to the apparitions is important because of their role as teachers in the Church. They have been generally quite favorable. Nevertheless, the objections of the Bishop of Mostar have accentuated their expression of reservation.

The Cardinal of Zagreb, Archbishop Kuharic, met with one of the girls in the group at Zagreb. I was assured that while she was with him she had an ecstasy. I do not know the date.

Bishop Franić, Archbishop of Split on the Dalmatian coast, went personally to Medjugorje very discreetly. Bishop Franić was a great friend of Cardinal Ottaviani and member of the doctrinal commissions of the Council, a man of tradition but not of rigidity. When he went to Medjugorje, he participated in the daily Rosary followed by the Mass. He was incognito among the people. He appreciated the quality of prayer at the liturgy. When the priest brought Communion to the faithful, he received along with them. The scarf with which he had covered over his Roman collar stopped anyone from recognizing him. In December 1983 he said to me what he had already said publicly: "Medjugorje has accomplished more in two years than our pastoral action has done in 40 years."

Concluding Remarks

Is it not a good indication that a sign from heaven would be given in a world where so often faith is relativized and evaporated in ideological abstractions, in a world where, for nearly 50 years, no apparition has been recognized? Is it surprising that the simplicity of these apparitions should appear childish, even contemptible, to the wisdom of the wise men of this age?

That this sign be given in a country of the East as an encouragement to those who defend their faith at the price of their personal interests and sometimes of their freedom (as the imprisonments arising from Medjugorje can witness) is also a happy sign of the times and Good News.

The unfinished symphony of Medjugorje requires that we be attentive to its last notes which will undoubtedly be, like the rest, notes of light but also of humility.

While reserving judgment to the episcopal authority responsible in this matter, and simply in my capacity and competence as an expert, well aware of my limits, I would say that my analysis leads me to a positive evaluation of the apparitions. The contrary indications seem to me to derive from unfortunate interferences and insufficient appreciation of an event which bears exceptional signs of being true.

I would only recall an important factor in this matter: the exceptional gift constituted by these apparitions is in no way the beatific vision, nor is it an absolute communication. It is a *sign* from heaven. And this is the reason why the Church keeps apparitions at a very humble level as pertaining to opinion and not to the certainty of faith. This lack of esteem for apparitions may have been excessive during the last centuries; it is, however, fundamentally justified. A balanced evaluation ought not to absolutize the apparitions and the words which are transmitted. There is always an element of the relative in the apparitions. The clothes that she adopts, which come from no department store, are relative. The same can be said about the color of her hair (black at Medjugorje) or her eyes or her age (18 to 20 years old at Medjugorje), younger or older elsewhere, her height (about 5 feet 4 inches at Medjugorje, almost a foot less at Lourdes). Glorified bodies have no age because they are outside cosmic time.

It makes no difference if the Virgin's robe was white, as at Lourdes, or "gray" or golden, according to the day, at Medjugorje. It makes no difference if she appears young at Lourdes where Bernanos recognized "the Virgin younger than sin" or if she appears as an adult elsewhere. An authentic apparition is true knowledge of the Virgin and true communication with her, even if she appears under signs and exterior trappings relative to each time, place, visionary, and particular message. If the inspired Scriptures which are the word of God have their own relativity according to the particular temperament of each sacred writer, then to a greater degree the apparitions have a relativity which ought to be evaluated with prudence and delicacy in each case and for each event. This relativity is due to the manner in which God and the Virgin, or any other Saint or servant of God, adapts to the one who beholds them and to the local situation. The relativity is also due to the living and normal interpretation of the communication made to each person.

There are other facts which also should be borne in mind. The Virgin appears simultaneously in different places. Since the 1981 school year, she appears to each of the young people in the town where they are studying: at Mostar, for Marija most often in the church; for Ivanka, in the girls' school; in Sarajevo for Mirjana, a student; at Dubrovnik for Ivan; while the apparitions continue in the room in the choir of the church for Vicka and Jakov.

When the young people are together and are in ecstasy, I have observed, after others, that sometimes many of them carry on a conversation with Our Lady at the same time. Such a thing would not be possible with someone of this world.

Such traits show the liberty of the glorified body. It is not, as we are, constrained to a succession of strictly limited acts nor to one place. The amazing instances of bilocation, seriously attested to in the lives of some saints, are an anticipation of this.

To say that the apparitions are a sign in no way implies that they are illusions. It is to say that they are not the end of the road but help for the journey. A sign functions to make known that which it signifies. Such is the case with every means of knowledge, for example, the image which appears on our television screen at the news hour. Such is the case with icons, means of transmitting a true encounter. It is the same, with due allowance being made, for the apparitions. Here, as well, knowledge is passed on through a sign, and the sign communicates the Reality from which it proceeds, in this case the Virgin Mary. Authentic visionaries are right in saying that they see, just as I say that I see the green tree and not the inverted image projected onto my retina.

Thomas Aquinas, aware of the humble status of faith and of language, said: "Faith terminates not in the concepts but in the reality signified by the concepts." That is, it terminates in God and in the mystery of salvation. In the same way the knowledge of those who behold apparitions does not terminate in the relative and temporary signs which are given to them. They gain access through the sign to a knowledge which is more vital, more direct. They gain access to a Presence. Their knowledge can be true, more true, more real, than ordinary knowledge, always, however, in keeping with the humble condition proper to such exceptional communication. They bear the mark of their earthly condition. The simplicity of the young people, the modesty with which they express themselves, illustrate this humble status which certain theologians or experts misunderstand sometimes. They either reduce the apparitions to a subjective experience or confer upon them an absolute character which goes beyond the reality of this temporal gift. The humility of the young people seems to me to be essential to the advancement of this movement of grace which necessarily will end by a return to the humble condition of faith. It will be lived on in the night, relying on traditional and sacramental signs of the Church.

The important thing is this new call of the Gospel which has been forgotten: prayer and conversion, with penance and fasting. As at the time of John the Baptist, it is an awakening to a living faith. In this way our world, being led by sin to its own destruction, can escape ruin. Only closed eyes are unable to understand the urgency of such a message.

Ivan

Ivanka and Vicka

Statue of Queen of Peace

Appendix 1:
Report Sent To Rome
By The Parish Of Medjugorje

The Urgency of the Message

Marija Pavlović had already arranged to have sent to the Pope a message in which the Blessed Virgin encouraged his work for peace. On November 30, 1983, she asked that a report be sent emphasizing the urgency of the message. The text of the report follows:

After the apparition of the Blessed Virgin on November 30, 1983, Marija Pavlović came to see me and said, "The Madonna says that the Supreme Pontiff and the Bishop must be advised immediately of the urgency and great importance of the message of Medjugorje".

This letter seeks to fulfill that duty.

1. Five young people (Vicka Ivanković, Marija Pavlović, Ivanka Ivanković, Ivan Dragicević, and Jakov Čolo) see an apparition of the Blessed Virgin every day. The experience in which they see her is a fact that can be checked by direct observation. It has been filmed. During the apparitions, the youngsters do not react to light, they do not hear sounds, they do not react if someone touches them, they feel that they are beyond time and space.

All of the youngsters basically agree that:

- "We see the Blessed Virgin just as we see anyone else. We pray with her, we speak to her, and we can touch her."
- "The Blessed Virgin says that world peace is at a critical stage. She repeatedly calls for reconciliation and conversion."
- "She has promised to leave a visible sign for all humanity at the site of the apparitions of Medjugorje."
- "The period preceding this visible sign is a time of grace for conversion and deepening of the faith."
- "The Blessed Virgin has promised to disclose ten secrets to us. So far, Vicka Ivanković has received eight. Marija Pavlović received the ninth one on December 8, 1983. Jakov Čolo, Ivan Dragicević and Ivanka Ivanković have each received nine. Only Mirjana Dragicević has received all ten."
- "These apparitions are the last apparitions of the Blessed Virgin on earth. That is why they are lasting so long and occurring so frequently."

2. The Blessed Virgin no longer appears to Mirjana Dragicević. The last time she saw one of the daily apparitions was Christmas, 1982. Since then, the apparitions have ceased for her, except on her birthday (March 18, 1983). Mirjana knew that this latter would occur.

According to Mirjana, the Madonna confided the tenth and last secret to her during the apparition of December 25, 1982. She also disclosed the dates on which the different secrets will come to pass. The Blessed Virgin has revealed to Mirjana many things about the future, more than to any of the other youngsters so far. For that reason I am reporting below what Mirjana told me during our conversation on November 5, 1983. I am summarizing the substance of her account, without word-for-word quotations. Mirjana said:

> Before the visible sign is given to humanity, there will be three warnings to the world. The warnings will be in the form of events on earth. Mirjana will be a witness to them. Three days before one of the admonitions, Mirjana will notify a priest of her choice. The witness of Mirjana will be a confirmation of the apparitions and a stimulus for the conversion of the world.
>
> After the admonitions, the visible sign will appear on the site of the apparitions in Medjugorje for all the world to see. The sign will be given as a testimony to the apparitions and in order to call people back to faith.
>
> The ninth and tenth secrets are serious. They concern chastisement for the sins of the world. Punishment is inevitable, for we cannot expect the whole world to be converted. The punishment can be diminished by prayer and penance, but it cannot be eliminated. Mirjana says that one of the evils that threatened the world, the one contained in the seventh secret, has been averted thanks to prayer and fasting. That is why the Blessed Virgin continues to encourage prayer and fasting: "You have forgotten that through prayer and fasting you can avert war and suspend the laws of nature."
>
> After the first admonition, the others will follow in a rather short time. Thus, people will have some time for conversion.
>
> That interval will be a period of grace and conversion. After the visible sign appears, those who are still alive will have little time for conversion. For that reason, the Blessed Virgin invites us to urgent conversion and reconciliation.
>
> The invitation to prayer and penance is meant to avert evil and war, but most of all to save souls.

According to Mirjana, the events predicted by the Blessed Virgin are near. By virtue of this experience, Mirjana proclaims to the world: "Hurry, be converted; open your hearts to God."

In addition to this basic message, Mirjana related an apparition she had in 1982 which we believe sheds some light on some aspects of Church history. She spoke of an apparition in which Satan appeared to her disguised as the Blessed Virgin. Satan asked Mirjana to renounce the Madonna and follow him. That way she could be happy in love and in life. He said that following the Virgin, on the contrary, would only lead to suffering. Mirjana rejected him, and immediately the Virgin arrived and Satan disappeared. Then the Blessed Virgin gave her the following message, in substance:

"Excuse me for this, but you must realize that Satan exists. One day he appeared before the throne of God and asked permission to submit the Church to a period of trial. God gave him permission to try the Church for one century. This century is under the power of the Devil, but when the secrets confided to you come to pass, his power will be destroyed. Even now he is beginning to lose his power and has become aggressive. He is destroying marriages, creating division among priests and is responsible for obsessions and murder. You must protect yourselves against these things through fasting and prayer, especially community prayer. Carry blessed objects with you. Put them in your house, and restore the use of holy water."

According to certain Catholic experts who have studied these apparitions, this message of Mirjana may shed light on the vision Pope Leo XIII had. According to them, it was after having had an apocalyptic vision of the future of the Church that Leo XIII introduced the prayer to St. Michael which priests used to recite after Mass up to the time of the Second Vatican Council. These experts say that the century of trials foreseen by Leo XIII is about to end.

Holy Father, I do not want to be responsible for the ruin of anyone. I am doing my best. The world is being called to conversion and reconciliation. In writing to you, Holy Father, I am only doing my duty. After drafting this letter, I showed it to the youngsters so that they might ask the Blessed Virgin whether its contents are accurate. Ivan Dragicević relayed the following answer: "Yes, the contents of the letter are the truth. You must notify first of all the Supreme Pontiff and then the Bishop."

This letter is accompanied by fasting and prayers that the Holy Spirit will guide your mind and your heart during this important moment in history.

Yours in the Sacred Hearts of Jesus and Mary,
Fr. Tomislav Vlašić
Medjugorje, December 2, 1983.

Appendix 2:
His Excellency Frane Franić
Archbishop of Split

The Archbishop had loaned his car to Fr. Robert Faricy, S.J., a professor at the Gregorian University of Rome, so that the latter could visit Medjugorje on December 11, 1981. After meeting with Fr. Faricy and hearing his favorable report, the Archbishop decided to go himself.

I arrived at the scene at 6:00 p.m. on December 19. It was already dark. The church was packed, and there was a line of cars coming from everywhere: Dubrovnik, Mostar, Sarajevo, even as far as Split. A large crowd was squeezed into the church, many young people. A Franciscan priest celebrated the Mass and gave a catechetical homily on faith as the source of confidence.

He spoke of miracles and their meaning, and he sounds like a man who really believes. He is obviously not contaminated by avant-garde theology. It was clear that he was favorably inclined to believe, though privately, of course, in the phenomena of Medjugorje. The people listened to him attentively. The church was full of young people, standing or kneeling. The liturgy followed the New Roman Missal.

Communion was distributed throughout the church by Franciscans in cassock and stole, but no surplice. I received Communion with the rest of the faithful. No one recognized me as a priest, because I hid my Roman collar under my scarf. I returned very pleased.

After Mass, there was prayer over the sick. No miracles occurred. It was not those who see the apparitions who prayed over the sick, but a Franciscan, along with several young girls who are probably members of the church's prayer group. After Mass, the youngsters who see the apparitions recited seven Our Father's. I saw them only from a distance, since I was in a pew in the middle of the church, among the rest of the faithful.

I hope that international experts like Frs. Beck and Faricy will be part of the Committee responsible for verifying the authenticity of the events of Medjugorje. (This account was published in Vijesnik: *The Messenger of the Diocese of Split*, 1982, No. 1, p. 24).

See pp. 14-15 (Ed. note: pp 19-20 of French copy) for documents in which Bishop Žanić of Mostar defended the apparitions against widespread slander by the press.

Appendix 3:
The Phenomena Of Light

Many witnesses allege having seen phemonena of light at various times in 1981:

1. Signs in the sun (August 2-4, 1981). I omit the testimony of Umberto Loncar, which was also published in the book by Kraljevic (pp. 98-99; see p. 57, where there is a disconcerting diversity in the testimonies).

2. On October 28, 1981, a large fire seemed to be burning on the hill. The hill was still under guard. Neither the police nor the firemen could find a trace of fire.

3. The following happened on October 21-22, 1981, and again on October 26, December 19, and other times. The cross of Križevac became a "column of light" and took on "the shape of a T". Then it gave way to a luminous girl, the Virgin Mary, who fits the description of the youngsters, but without being as clearly defined. The first two times it occurred—during the trial of the Pastor, Fr. Jozo Zovko—the phenomenon was longer (about half an hour). Subsequent occurrences lasted 15-20 minutes. Many people saw it, from various locations and at different angles.

The Bishop has heard it said that there were precedents last century, but the local people remember nothing of that. A critical study needs to be made of these unusual phenomena. Here are a few testimonies.

Anka Pehar

On Thursday evening, September 15, 1981, I had gone outside to take in the clean clothes hanging on the line. The sky was cloudless, but it was already dark. Above the hill of Crnica, I saw a funnel-shaped light; that is, the light rose from the ground increasing in width as it got higher. Then I saw, in this light, Our Lady, with her arms spread wide. She floated in the air and was headed in the direction of the church in Medjugorje.

I called my daughter Nada so that she, too could see it. She came out of the house and saw the same thing I did. Then we called our grandmother, Anica. She saw it, too. A little while later, Kata Pehar and her daughter Dalia, a child of nine, joined us. We were all kneeling and praying, and all of us saw what I did. Our Lady was surrounded by light, but the brightest rays came from behind her head and shoulders. This lasted almost an hour. We saw Our Lady move from the hill of Crnica in the direction of the church of Medjugorje. She was wearing an exquisite cape with a hood. Later, Our Lady disappeared and the light went out. She disappeared before reaching the church.

An illusion? No, I was not the only one to see it. There were five of us and we all saw the same thing. With me were: Nada (my daughter); Kata; Dalia Pehar (9 years old); Anica (the grandmother).

Anka Pehar
Gradnici, October 17, 1981

Brother Janko Buballo

On October 22, 1981, I had come to Medjugorje. I was in the rectory, awaiting Mass time. A little after 5 p.m. I heard an unusual disturbance in the house. Two sisters who take care of the church and the rectory were running through the house. I found myself near the window, in the office of the rectory. I looked outside and saw the two nuns kneeling on the damp ground, their arms opened wide. With them were some 70 men and women, all on their knees, forming a line that extended up to the church. Apparently, no one was worried about the rain. No umbrellas. Everyone was praying and entreating. Some were crying with emotion, others were singing hymns. All had their eyes turned toward the cross on the hill of Križevac.

I also looked toward the cross, but it had disappeared. In its place was a strange light, pale pink, unlike anything in real life.

I was touched. Since I do not have good eyesight, I asked for a pair of binoculars to look at it. Someone gave me Brother Tomislav's. I adjusted them to my eyesight. Then I saw, in place of the cross, the silhouette of a woman. She was opening her arms. Her head reached a bit above the vertical beam of the cross. Her feet were hidden in a luminous cloud near the base of the cross.

Let's be clear: the details—like the face, the eyes, the hair—I could not see. While looking at this sight, I was filled with great joy. There were four of five priests with me. We all saw the same thing. So did others in the village. Everyone who, at that moment, looked toward the cross on Križevac hill saw it. The phenomenon lasted about 40 minutes.

Eager to understand the meaning of this phenomenon, those who witnessed it asked the youngsters to seek an explanation from the Blessed Virgin. She confirmed that it was she who was on the hill.

Brother Stanko Vasilj

At about 4:30 p.m. on October 22, 1981, I arrived in Medjugorje to help in the parish. With me were Brothers Luka Susac, Vinko Dragicević and Janko Buballo. All four of us are from the monastery of Humac. After a brief stop at the rectory, I headed for the church to see if it was necessary to prepare the faithful for confession. I found 60 to 70 people.

I went to the sacristy to collect what is necessary for the new ritual. Sister Ignacia Bebekj, who is in charge of catechism, was in the sacristy. While awaiting the arrival of the faithful, I went outside. The rain had stopped, but the sky was still dark. Looking toward the hill of Križevac, I noticed that the cross had disappeared! I looked a second time: yes, the cross of Križevac had really disappeared. Astonished, I wanted to go back inside the sacristy. But before entering, I looked once against toward the hill. Instead of the cross, I saw a white column. I went into the sacristy and said to the sister: "Come out, Sister, and see this." She answered: "Look, Our Lady! Yesterday, the residents of Miletina saw her several times at the same spot!"

I looked up again in the direction of Križevac. I saw the same white column. I then returned to the rectory to tell the other Franciscans who came with me, as well as Fr. Tomislav Vlašić.

On the way, between the well and the rectory, I met Brother Vinko and two nuns. They looked in the direction of Križevac. I asked them if they saw anything. Brother Vinko answered, "You're not blind, are you? Don't you see it?"

At that moment I noticed three other Franciscans at the window of the office in the rectory. They, too, were looking toward Krizevać. On entering the office, I saw that Brother Luka had binoculars in his hands. I snatched them out of his hands and turned them in the direction of the hill. After a quick adjustment, I exclaimed, "There she is!"

What did I see? In place of the white column, I saw the silhouette of a woman dressed in a gray cloak, a gray that was very soft and luminous, somewhat like a neon light. At a certain moment, a sparkling ray of light shone from her right cheek. Brother Luka took back the binoculars. I hurried back to the church to inform the faithful. But as I was coming out, I saw all the people kneeling behind the church, facing east. They were singing, praying and shouting joyfully with excitement. Drawing closer, I heard the following exclamation, which stuck in my memory. It was made by Milka Korac, from the village of Hamzici: "Oh, thank you Mary! Tonight is the 15th time that you have come. Thank you for being able to see you. Now, let anything that you wish happen in my life."

Similar exclamations were heard amidst the prayers and hymns. The ground was soaked with mud, but all were on their knees.

While the faithful were praying and singing, a van from Split arrived in front of the church. In it were three Carmelite priests and four nuns. They joined our prayers. When we got up, those who had arrived from Split told us that they had observed the phenomenon ever since Tromedja, a distance of a little over a mile. They were happy to have seen all of this. One of the nuns made this remark, "As for me, I didn't see anything, neither on the road nor here."

Here is how the phenomenon ended. First of all a cloud arose, at the spot where the cross normally is. The cloud was clear and transparent. It was split in two, shaped like a fan. Then another cloud, thick and dark, descended like a heavy curtain on both sides of the cross. Finally, the cross appeared, looking as it always does gray concrete made darker by the rain which soaked it.

Full of joy, we returned to the church to pray, and to go to confession or to hear confessions.

I declare that all of the above is true, fully conscious of my weighty responsibility before God and the Church.

Humac, November 17, 1982
Brother Stanko Vasilj

Appendix 4:
Healings At Medjugorje?

Are healings occurring at Medjugorje? Many people claim to have been healed. Some inform the parish, and, of these, some leave supporting medical documentation. Father Rupčić has published 55 cases of healings. These are spontaneous witnesses usually without any supporting documentation.

In our Western world, the publication of first-hand claims such as these might be surprising. We are used to the publication of healings only when these are verified by extensive examinations, both medical and religious in nature. The published healings at Medjugorje remind us more of the records compiled in the 19th century by the doctor at Saint-Maclou, who was the first to be concerned with on-the-spot verification. He attached importance to a sort of "law of large numbers" rather than to extensive in-depth verification of a single case.

The 55 cases published by Father Rupčić were given to Dr. Mangiapan, chief of the medical bureau at Lourdes. He summarized these in two ways.

First, the medical statistics:

- 8 cases of eye (3) and ear (5) disease
- 2 cases of arthritic disease (not of much interest)
- 6 cases of vascular disease (cerebral 5, cardiac 3)
- 1 case of neurological disease
- 4 cases of wounds or disease of the limbs, usually lower limbs; (2 wounds, 2 varicose veins)
- 4 cases of general illness
- 4 cases of tumors
- 1 case of kidney disease

Second, with respect to quality of information, there are:

- 16 cases with no diagnosis at all
- 9 cases with insufficient or strange diagnoses (These 25 cases are not considered further here)
- 31 cases have a pathology which is more or less identifiable.

Even so, further inquiry would be needed to establish: (1) the precise nature of the illness; (2) its seriousness (not always obvious); (3) its duration or likely duration (in relation to a possibly natural but spontaneous healing); and (4) its possible response to normal medical treatment already being received.

As a result of discussions with Dr. Patrick Mahéo, of Rennes, we consider 30 of the latter cases here. Some people will not take this collection of data very seriously, but without some evidence of the healings taking place at Medjugorje it would be impossible to convey a complete idea of what is taking place there. These testimonies, though not fully confirmed, and in no way "official," introduce us to faithful believers, to those used to signs, and to concrete manifestations of God's presence. One must not be too quick to label these attitudes superstitious. The testimonies remind us of the Gospel. They are from people who believe and hope in the same realistic way that so impressed Jesus and so filled him with joy and admiration. Their witness is simple, like that of the man born blind when faced with the Pharisees' derision: "I know only this, I was blind, but now I see" (Jn. 9:25).

At Medjugorje, parishioners and pilgrims both experience a renewal in their relationship with God. They come to know him as a God concerned with small everyday happenings in their lives, as well as with major and significant events. This link with God is a source of real happiness.

In selecting these healings we have used criteria suitable for the confirmation of miracles. But this should not make us forget that many spiritual healings may be excluded by these criteria. Here are some examples of such spiritual healings quite properly listed by Father Rupčić:

- I was a confirmed alcoholic. In spite of my own efforts and many treatments, I couldn't stop drinking. I stopped the day after going to Medjugorje. (There are several cases like this).
- I was addicted to smoking and couldn't stop. After I prayed at Medjugorje I was able to stop with no problem. (Nada Sulic)
- I had a real phobia of traveling. No doctor was able to help me. This simply disappeared after I went to Medjugorje. (Ruža Stoljić)
- I used to be afflicted with muscular twitching in my face. Everyone called me the "blinker". I couldn't control it. (Ivan Frančić).

151

The next series of reports relates to organic or physical healings. They had been submitted to the necessary verification.

Jozo Vasilj (born in 1896 at Medjugorje)

Eight years ago I had a stroke which rendered my left eye completely useless. During the past four years my right eye also stopped functioning and I couldn't see anymore. I asked Vida Vasilj to bring some flowers and sage from the Crnica hill. That same night I put these plants under my head. In the morning I asked my wife to bring me water. I put the plants in the water and washed myself. Upon drying myself with a towel, I said to my wife "There, I can see!" She answered me, "What do you mean you can see?" I said to her, "I can see you haven't put your socks on yet!" That is how my wife found out I could really see. While I was washing I recited the Creed.

Another time I was in our church; it was was when Jure Ivanković came from the U.S.A. Once again, God gave me a great grace. For some time my hands had been covered with open sores which were very painful; they disappeared that very day. These things happened in the early days of the apparitions.

Deposition taken by Father Stanko Vasilj, September 14, 1981.

Matija Skuban (Lassale Strasse, Karlsruhe 21, West Germany)

"I was a paraplegic after a stroke. During prayer on July 20, 1981, in the church at Medjugorje, I felt something like a strong current all through my body, and especially in my bad left leg. I got up for communion."

Up to this time, Matija Skuban needed someone to help her up. She had already had three operations. Her left leg and arm were paralyzed.

On March 1, 1982 she wrote an account of her healing. She also brought medical certificates dated January 4, and February 18, 1982.

Antonija Puljic (of Podvinje)

Antonija, a little girl two years old, was badly burned. Her doctor said she would not be able to walk for a month and a half. Her parents went to the place of the apparitions and prayed for her. That same evening she began to walk. Two days later the burned areas were healed over, and she was healed.

Medical certificates were given.

Marja Sarić (born February 7, 1960 at Andrijevci)

Marja had a tumor on her knee. She was treated in a hospital in Belgrade but after surgery her condition became worse. The doctors considered amputation of the leg. Meanwhile, her mother had made a vow to the Holy Virgin to obtain her healing. The mother went to Medjugorje where she asked God and Our Lady for health for her daughter. The young people also prayed for her. Before the mother's return, her daughter was completely healed. The healing occurred at the end of October, 1981.

It was announced on September 27, 1982 when mother and daughter returned to Medjugorje to thank Our Lady.

Cvija Kuzman (from Stolac)

Cvija suffered for eleven years from degenerative arthritis. She had been treated in hospitals at Stolac, Mostar, and Čapljina. Thanks to these treatments she could walk, but her arms and legs remained swollen and painful. On the eve of the feast of the Assumption, August 15, 1981, Cvija went to the hill of the apparitions. She brought back a little earth, which she put in water. Her daughter washed her with this, reciting seven times the Our Father, the Hail Mary, the Glory Be to the Father and the Creed. She was completely healed. Before her healing she had prayed in honor of Our Lady. Afterward, she promised to fast regularly.
Deposition, August 29, 1981.

Sr. Božidara Čupić (of Metković)

Sr. Čupić suffered from kidney problems for a long time, and also had an ear infection. For three months she was deaf in one ear. For several years she had been treated by doctors from Dubrovnik, but without success.

She recited the prayers recommended by Our Lady. Her healing was instantaneous and complete.

She promised to bring documents on her state of health, before and after.
Deposition collected in August, 1981.

Ivan Jukić (a boy from Posusje)

Ivan had sores all over his body for six months. These would form very irritating scabs. After bathing, these scabs would hurt even more, and the child would scream from the pain. His parents took him to dermatologists at Posusje and Listica, but without any success. On July 25, they soaked flowers from the hill of the apparitions in water. They said seven times the Our Father, Hail Mary, Glory Be to the Father, and the Creed. After the prayers they washed the boy with the water. The next day, the scabs, red blotches, and itching were gone; the child was peaceful and did not cry. This had rarely happened before. The healing has continued to the present time.

To thank Our Lady, the parents promised to go to Medjugorje on foot. *Deposition October 15, 1981.*

Dubravko Tomašic (Ludwigsburg, West Germany)

Dubravko went to Medjugorje and was healed of leukemia. His parents have promised to present medical documents.

Anica Brekalo (born March 23, 1920 at Split)

Anica suffered from blood clots in her legs and also from degenerative rheumatism. She had been treated in a hospital at Split, with no relief. She made a vow to go to Medjugorje. In preparation, she prayed and fasted regularly. During the communal prayer for the sick at Medjugorje, she felt herself getting better. Afterwards the sickness simply disappeared. Now, according to her own words, she is completely healed.

Božica Sušac (of Ljubuški)

Božica suffered for a long time from an open sore on her chest. Doctors were unable to give her relief. She took some herbs from the hill of the apparitions and soaked these in water. She washed the sore with this water. The sore healed over two or three days later, and has not reappeared.

Ilka Bazina (from Mostar)

Ilka detected a small tumor, the size of a hazel-nut, in her left breast. Her brother, a doctor, sent her to a hospital in Sarajevo. After a biopsy, an operation was suggested. She asked what the results might be. Her doctor replied, "I'm not God, only he knows."

Ilka refused the operation. Instead she went on foot to Medjugorje. There she prayed, went to confession and to communion. On the way home she realized that the "hazel-nut" in her breast had disappeared. To be sure, her brother sent her back to the hospital at Sarajevo. The doctors there declared her to be healed. Ilka has no pain, and the tumor is gone. She submitted medical documents on May 8, 1982.

Ante Stolčić (Leidisstadt Hotel, 799 Friedrichshafen (WestGermany, born in 1951 on the island of Rab)

Ante's kidneys no longer functioned, and he was on a regular schedule of dialysis. He was healed at Medjugorje. He has promised to submit all the needed documents.

Danijel Šétka (of Mostar)

Danijel's three year old child contracted septicemia four days after his birth and was paralyzed for 16 days. Afterwards the paralysis diminished, but half of the boy's body did not develop normally. He was unable to walk without help. He fell often. He could only say one or two stammered words. The six young people told his parents he would be healed if they had faith.

His mother often came to pray at Medjugorje and she took some earth from the hill of the apparitions. The child was prayed over in the church. At the beginning of November, 1981, his mother declared that the child was healed.

She said that the healing has been taking place gradually and that she would be happy even if he were to stay as he now is, except she would like his arm to have more mobility.

Formerly the boy had been treated at the hospital in Mostar. His parents had also obtained medication for him from West Germany, but nothing had produced any results. This healing created a sensation.

Luca Prusina (of Čitluk)

Luca had suffered for five or six years from an ear infection. Treatments at Čitluk and Ljubuški were without results. Luca prayed and fasted. She also took flowers from the hill of the apparitions, soaked them in water and washed her ears with the mixture.

To the present time (November 14, 1981) she has had no pain.

Lucija Raspudić (from Djakovo)

Lucija had cataracts and could no longer see. She had been treated at Djakovo and Osijek with no success. She went to the hill of the apparitions, picked some flowers and took a little earth. She put these in water and washed her eyes with the preparation. She made a vow to Our Lady, and when she accomplished it the cataracts disappeared. This was in September, 1981.

Her statement was received in December, and she has promised to provide medical reports.

Jure Bošnjak (of Mostar)

Jure had a stroke. He received medical care at Mostar and Banja Luka, but did not improve. He was hospitalized at Mostar, and thus could not go to pray or attend services at Medjugorje. However, his family took his clothes there and the priest blessed them. Afterwards Jure prayed and got better while he was in the hospital at Mostar. His healing is complete.

Iva Tole (born in 1941 at Mostar)

Iva had multiple sclerosis. She was treated in hospitals in Belgrade and Zagreb, but did not improve. She retired prematurely due to the disability, and stayed at home. Her condition became continually worse. She wanted to go to "Our Lady's home" at Medjugorje, but was not strong enough, so her daughter went for her. There the daughter prayed, fasted, and asked little Jakov if her mother would get better. He told her, "If she believes, fasts, and prays, her health will improve."

Finally on September 13, 1981 the woman herself was brought to the Church at Medjugorje. She prayed, and then went on foot to the Križevac Hill to hear Mass. She returned home full of joy. Her headaches have disappeared. She now does the housework; something she had no longer been able to do. She declared her healing on May 20, 1982, and deposited the relevant medical documents.

Božica Mandić (of Ljubuški)

Bozica had degenerative arthritis. She had been treated by a doctor in Ljubuški. After nine pilgrimages on foot to Medjugorje, and daily recitation of seven Our Father's, she was completely healed.

Ljubica Meržo (of Mostar)

Ljubica had suffered a long time from angina. With a strong faith, she prayed and fasted. After a pilgrimage to Medjugorje the angina completely disappeared.

She declared her healing on January 19, 1982.

Anda Marić (of Sinj)

Anda had an accident while cutting ears of corn. She had cut her eye and could no longer see out of it. She suffered a great deal, but did not want to consult a doctor. Her husband went to Medjugorje and brought back some plants from the hill of the apparitions. Anda rinsed her eye in water containing the soaked plants, and she prayed.

She says that she could see right away. The pain is gone.
Deposition taken by Tomislav Pervan, February 5, 1982.

Katica Mikola (of Osijek)

Katica had a stroke, and her mind had been disturbed for two and a half years. She had been treated at the psychiatric hospital of Osijek, without improvement. Her family made a vow, and went to Medjugorje. They took a little earth and some flowers from the hill of the apparitions, having prayed and fasted beforehand. When their vow was fulfilled on Christmas Eve, 1981, Katica was instantly healed.

On January 19, she went to her doctor who declared her to be in a perfect state of health.

This declaration was made by Katica's family on January 31, 1982. They promised to send medical documents.

Vinka Marinčić (of Čitluk)

Vinka had a cerebral hemorrhage. She was treated at Mostar and Zagreb. She made a vow to Our Lady, and prayed and fasted. While on pilgrimage to Medjugorje, she took some earth from the hill of the apparitions. She was healed instantly after praying to the Blessed Virgin Mary. *Deposition received in early February, 1982.*

Jure Bjelić (of Opuzen)

Jure had a major ear infection. An operation in 1954 had been unsuccessful. He lost his hearing, and the wound remained open, discharging pus. Doctors stated that a new operation offered the only hope for healing, but that there was no guarantee the operation would be successful. Jure refused the operation. On September 13, 1981, while attending Mass on the Križevac hill, he was healed. Prior to this he had prayed, fasted, and carried about with him some earth from the hill of the apparitions. His ear no longer has a discharge, the pains are gone, and he hears better.

He made this declaration on February 20, 1982. He promised to submit the relevant medical documents.

Vlado Grizelj (of Ljubuški)

Vlado had a chronic ear infection. He had been treated in hospitals at Ljubuški and Mostar, but without success. During the summer of 1981, he made a pilgrimage with his parents to Medjugorje. They took some flowers from the hill of the apparitions, soaked them in water and washed his ear with the mixture. They made a vow, and prayed over him in the church. He was healed instantly; the illness has not recurred.

This declaration was made by his parents at the beginning of March 1982.

Ante Kozina (of Čitluk)

Ante had suffered from a chronic ear infection since 1942. He received treatment in Mostar and West Germany. The doctors in Germany suggested surgery, warning him of the risks. He refused the operation. His ear hurt a great deal and was discharging pus.

In October 1981, Ante made a vow in the church of Medjugorje, and was instantly healed. He has not suffered since that time.
Deposition, March 12, 1982.

Mirko Brkič (of Banja Luka)

Mirko broke his leg and a pin was placed in it. He was treated first in a hospital in Banja Luka and then in Belgrade. An open sore, under the knee of the broken leg, was treated many times, but the sore became deeper until the bone was visible. Doctors decided to amputate. Meanwhile Mirko's family had made a vow to Our Lady, and prayed and fasted. The day before the scheduled amputation, the wound suddenly closed. The astonished doctors cancelled the operation. After several days the wound was completely healed over.

The healing was made public on March 26, 1982.

Venka Bilič-Brajčić (of Split)

The diagnosis was as follows:

In January, 1980, the patient had her left breast removed, and afterward, she received postoperative radiation treatment. Nine months after the operation there were numerous metastases. These had reached the right breast on which radiation treatment began in April, 1981.

Venka herself reported: "In the month of September, 1981, the scabs on my breast became sores: at first many little ones, which then became first one, then two large sores. My sister said that Our Lady of Medjugorje could help me, and suggested that I pray to her. At first we prayed at home. Then my sister arranged with some other women to pray in the church. Two or three days after this prayer the appearance of the sores started to change. The scabs fell off and new skin began to form. During January the lower sore disappeared, and the upper one also dried up. My health is better."

The disease is in remission. Venka feels well, and the medical certificate confirms that there is no sign of further metastases into the bone or other organs.

Venka returned to Medjugorje to thank Our Lady. She submitted medical documents on September 8, 1982.A hypnotic test of the

A Hypnotic Test Of The Sincerity Of The Young People Who See The Apparitions.

Dr. Ludvik Stopar, psychiatrist and para-psychologist was trained at Graz and Berlin (psychiatry and hypnotherapy) as well as at Freiburg-im-Breisgau (para-psychology). For fifteen years he was director of the "Polyclinic of Maribor" in Yugoslavia. He put Marija Pavlović under hypnosis in order to test her sincerity. First, he had her give an account of the apparitions while she was completely conscious. Then he had her give an account while under hypnosis. The latter was given in an expressionless voice. There were no disagreements except that, in contrast to the account given while conscious, Marija spoke without hesitation while under hypnosis. Also, under hypnosis, Marija told the secret she had kept while conscious. Dr. Stopar has kept this strictly to himself as required by his professional code. To him, her sincerity appears fully established.

During four visits, each of which lasted about a week, from May, 1982 to November, 1983, Dr. Stopar examined the young people in their normal state and while they were in ecstasy.

Appendix 5:
Chronological Landmarks

1981

June 24, Wednesday: First apparition, still hazy, to two, then to six youths.

June 25, Thursday: (*6:15 p.m., which will become the usual hour*) Second apparition, to the definitive group of six young people.

June 26, Friday: The person in the apparition gives her identity: "I am the Blessed Virgin Mary." She also gave the key theme of the message: "Peace, peace, peace! Reconcile yourselves."

June 27, Saturday: First interrogation by the police at Čitluk. Then, the fourth apparition.

June 28, Sunday: Fifth apparition. 15,000 people are present. Our Lady looked at the crowd and smiled.

June 29, Monday: Sixth apparition. Invitation to faith: "There is only one God, one faith." The young people ask for the healing of little Danijel Setka, whose healing will take place gradually (see above).

June 30, Tuesday: Seventh apparition at Cerno, on the way back from the "ride" on which the young people had been taken to keep them away from the place of the apparitions.

July 2: Establishment of daily Mass at the parish church; timed to follow the apparitions.

July 13:	Police limit access to the hill. The apparitions begin to take place discreetly and privately.
August 6:	The word *Mir* (peace) is written in the sky.
August 7:	Our Lady calls the young people to the mountain at 2 a.m. and asks that penance be done for sinners.
August 15:	A large crowd of people come to Medjugorje. The police and authorities are worried.
August 17:	The pastor, Fr. Jozo Zovko is arrested and imprisoned.
August 18:	The assistant, Fr. Zrinko Cuvalo, another Franciscan, becomes pastor. Fr. Tomislav Vlašić is named assistant.
End of August:	During an apparition in the village of Bijakovići, Mary says: "I am the Queen of Peace."
October 21-22:	The trial of Fr. Jozo Zovko who is sentenced to two and one half years in prison.
1982	
January 14:	Henceforth the apparitions take place in the church, in the room opposite the sacristy, after the rosary and before Mass.
August 20:	The second pastor, Fr. Zrinko Cuvalo, resigns and Fr. Tomislav Pervan becomes pastor.
December 15:	Helena and Mirjana receive a charism by which they "see by means of the heart" and receive messages.

December 25:   Mirjana receives the tenth secret which she alone knows. She reverts to an ordinary state of faith. There remain now only five young people who see the apparitions.

1983
February 17:   Fr. Jozo Zovko is released from prison after having served a year and a half of his sentence.

December 25:   The Virgin, in a golden robe, appears with the child Jesus as on the previous August 15.

Appendix 6:
Access To Medjugorje

Airports: The nearest are at Mostar (18 miles, summer only), Dubrovnik, Split, and Sarajevo (about 60 miles from Medjugorje, but because of the winding roads actually more than 80 miles).

Trains: From Zagreb (on the main trans-European line), go to Sarajevo then Mostar. Then to Čitluk: 3 miles from Medjugorje.

Roads: From Zagreb, two possible routes:
- 285 miles by way of Okučani, Banja Luka, Jajce, Bugojno, Gornji Vakuf, Jablanica, Mostar.
- 300 miles by Karlovac, Bihać, Bosanski Petrovač, Titov Drvar, Bosansko Grahovo, Livno, Imotski, Ljubuski.
  This way, though longer, is recommended: seven hours instead of eight.

From Split: Go to Ljubuški then Čitluk.Turn right one mile before Čitluk.

From Dubrovnik: Go to Ljubuški by way of Metković and Čapljina. Then, as above.

There are hotels at Mostar (about 20 miles), Čapljina (17 miles), Ljubuški (12 miles), Čitluk (3 miles). Price: 20 German Marks or 720 dinars at Čitluk. The Marxist government can not officially authorize pilgrimages. However, they allow tourists who, on an individual basis and with respect for the civil order, go to Medjugorje to pray.

Appendix 7:
It Happened In Yugoslavia
In The Croatian Region Of Hercegovina

A Kaleidoscope

Yugoslavia is a composite country, bordering on Italy, Austria, Hungary, Romania, Bulgaria, Greece and Albania, and on the Adriatic, along the beautiful Dalmatian coast. It comprises 159,880 square miles and numbers 22,350,000 people.

It is a kaleidoscopic federation, subject to severe tensions. Five nationalities are officially recognized: Serbs, Croats, Slovenes, Macedonians, and Montenegrans. To those we might add the Moslem Croats, who date back to the Turkish era and were granted the status of "Moslem nationality" in 1960, and 18 ethnic minorities. The largest of the latter group are the Albanians and Hungarians, concentrated in Kosovo and Vojvodina, respectively.

There are 6 republics: Bosnia-Hercegovina (capital: Sarajevo); Croatia (Zagreb); Macedonia (Skopje); Montenegro (Titograd); Slovenia (Ljubljana); and Serbia (Belgrade). Serbia encompasses the two autonomous regions of Kosovo and Vojvodina.

Fourteen languages are spoken: Serbian, Croatian, Slovenian, Macedonian, Hungarian, Albanian, Montenegran, Turkish, Rumaninan, Italian, German, Slovak, Bulgarian, and Greek. Only four of these are official languages: Croatian, Macedonian, Serbian, and Slovenian.

Two alphabets are used: Latin and Cyrillic.

There is only one political party: Communist.

World War II

During World War II, Yugoslavia was torn apart by totalitarian extremists from both ends of the spectrum. Hitler occupied the country and cultivated the most radical right-wing elements, while Tito fought as a Marxist on the atheistic left wing. The war saw 1,700,000 killed out of a total population of 15 million. All of the old antagonisms were heightened during the struggle, and, thus many wounds and irresolvable tensions remain. That explains why the Yugoslav regime, while in many ways more open than other countries of the East bloc, nonetheless holds the record for the proportion of political prisoners, according to *Amnesty International*.

On November 29, 1945, a victorious Tito established the *Federal Republic of Yugoslavia*, governed by the Constitution of January 1946. The practice of religion falls under the principle of separation of Church and State, a principle tempered somewhat by Tito's re-establishment of diplomatic relations with the Holy See in 1966 and the opening of a nunciature. And we have seen this atheistic state adopt a religious class (Moslem) to designate one of its nationalities. The country remains 87% religious.

The Religions

Yugoslavia is a mosaic of religious denominations that is unique in Europe and indeed in the world:

Orthodox:	13,700,000
Catholics:	7,715,000
Moslems:	2,319,000
Protestants:	220,000
Jews:	7,800
Other faiths:	2,000

In addition:

No religious beliefs:	1,900,000
Atheists:	1,343,000

The Catholics are mainly Croats and Slovenes.

The Croats, who account for two-thirds of the Catholic population, are distributed as follows:

4,000,000 in Croatia
  800,000 in Bosnia-Hercegovina, *(where Medjugorje is located).*
  200,000 in Serbia
5,000,000 Croatian Catholics throughout Yugoslavia
2,500,000 emigrants
7,500,000 total Croatian Catholics in the world.

The Croatian Story

The name Croat is mentioned as far back as the 6th century B.C. in the inscription on the tomb of Darius. The name was the source of the French word *cravate* (necktie). Many of the Croatian young men exiled during the Turkish occupation served in the French army. They wore a piece of light cloth around their neck and were referred to as "cravate cavaliers."

The Croatians, coming from the East, swept down the Carpathian mountains towards the Adriatic. They were evangelized in the 7th century, making them the first Slavic people to adopt Christianity. The Croatian church has maintained its deep traditions and vitality throughout a history marked by terrible trials. The Church has passed through successive and intense phases of independence and oppression, amid struggles and persecutions that were often bloody.

Bosnia was placed in the care of the Franciscans, who distinguished themselves during the Islamic persecution and still enjoy great prestige. In 1881, Pope Leo XIII installed the normal secular hierarchy. This change deprived the Franciscans of their unique position and, over time, deprived them of a number of parishes where very strong bonds had been established. Tensions rose in the Church during the 1960's when the increase of vocations to the secular clergy accelerated the transfer of parishes to the diocesan priests. This local problem, aggravated in the diocese of Mostar, led to troublesome and deceptive confusion in the matter of the apparitions of Medjugorje.

Medjugorje

The parish of Medjugorje (3,400 people) includes the hamlets of Bijakovići, Miletina, Vionica and Surmanci. Tobacco, grape vines and wheat are grown there. Clusters of Canaan grapes weighing up to eight pounds have been harvested. The inhabitants live in a close covenant with God, seeing sun and rain as tokens and signs of his gifts. They are conscious of the fact that except for God, no one has brought anything to this country other than rape and violence. The level of education and culture is unusually high.

It is a classic, traditional peasant parish. Although the faith had grown somewhat lukewarm because of the general condition of the world, the apparitions have touched off an unprecedented renewal of fervor that is surely unique in the world.

Since 1933, the parish is overlooked by the large cross (Kriz) of Sipovac Hill. The hill is about 1,500 feet high and has become known as Križevac. The feast day is observed every year on the Sunday following September 8th. In 1982, 70,000 pilgrims came, and in 1983, 100,000.

Appendix 8:
Bibliography

Archives

Archives from the Parish of Medjugorje, the Diocese of Mostar, the Yugoslav Police and Government are secret, not open to the public.

Reports In Manuscript Form

Barbarić, Slavko, *Examen psycho-pedagogique des voyants de Medjugorje*. A manuscript report kept in the archives of the parish of Medjugorje. This is a psycho-sociological study of the group of six young people. It demonstrates that their unity, cohesiveness, and interrelations cannot be explained in terms of their individual characteristics or endowments. These derive from that to which the group has reference, namely the apparitions. Rupčić and Kraljević use these arguments and conclusions in a parallel and faithful manner.

Cali, Roland, *Les apparitions de Sainte Marie en Europe de l'Est, ou Notre Dame de Medjugorje (Yougoslavie)*. An account of a journey made in December, 1982 by the author and Fr. M. Korjek, 5 pages.

Stopar, (Dr. Ludvik), neuro-psychiatrist and parapsychologist, theist. *Relation de decembre 1982*. A report of his examination of the young people under hypnosis, concluding that they are completely sincere.
Kršni Zavičaj, No. 16, Hercegovina; 1983, (in Croatian) pp. 160-213. Witnesses Of Graces Received And Of Healings.
Rainha da Paz. Una nova Fatima na Jugoslavia, (Queen of Peace, a new Fatima in Yugoslavia). Braga, Boa Nova, 2nd edition, 1983, 190 pages. Three other brochures of 190 pages, for Portuguese pilgrims, same publishers.
Medjugorje et la Sainte Vierge Reine de la Paix, Paris, Tequi, 1984, 32 pages.

Books

Buballo, Janko, *Medjugorje, interview des voyants.* Unpublished manuscript, consulted in Yugoslavia.

Kraljevič, Svetozar, *Le village a l'heure de la vierge.* This book has been translated and adapted by Ephraim Croissant and Philippe Madre: *Les apparitions de Medjugorje,* Fayard, 1984, 128 pages. It has also been edited in English by Fr. Michael Scanlan of the University of Steubenville under the title *The Apparitions of Mary at Medjugorge,* Chicago: Franciscan Herald Press, 1984, 224 pages.

Ljubić, Marijan, *Erscheinungen der Gottesmutter in Medjugorje,* Jestetten, Miriam-Verlag, 1983, 176 pages. This has been translated into French, under the title *La Vierge Marie apparait en Yougoslavie,* Hauteville (Suisse), Editions du Parvis, 1984, 166 pages.

L. Rooney and R. Faricy, *Maria regina della pace,* Milano, Ancora, 1983, 96 pages. This will soon appear in a French translation and is published in English under the title *Mary, Queen of Peace,* New York, Alba House, 1984.

Rupčić, Ljudevit, *Gospena Ukazanja u Medjugorje (The apparitions of Our Lady at Medjugorje),* Samobor, A. G. Matos, 1983, 172 pages.

Triclot, P. *Notre Dame de la paix en Yougoslavie,* 59790 Ronchin, ed. J. Hovine, 1984, 106 pages. An illustrated account of a pilgrimage made February 5-6, 1984.

Zanon, Giovanni, Medjugorje. *La Madonna parla ancora,* Padua, April Can be obtained from the author, via Aurelio Baruzzi 7, 35100 Padova, Italy. The book repeats the investigation of Fr. Rupčić (without citing him) and other documents.

Articles In Chronological Order

Glas Koncila (The Voice of the Council). A bi-monthly Catholic Croatian publication which contained a long series of well-informed articles, beginning with July 12, 1981.

Pavlović, Pavle, an article which appeared in the Croatian periodical *Arena,* July 22, 1981, pp. 46-47. It contains much useful information.

Vlašić, Ferdo, an important series of articles in *Naša Ognjišta (Our Homes),* October, 1981 to April, 1982. These articles resulted in the sentencing of the 63-year-old author, who is also editor-in-chief of the periodical. He was sentenced to eight years in prison which was later reduced to five. His secretary, Joza Krizic, 32 years old, was sentenced to two and one half years. The periodical had to change its name to *Sveta Baština*, (*Holy Heritage*).

"Sterne auf der Stirn. Eine Marienerscheinung bei einem Dorf in Herzegovina lockt Pilgermassen und bedroht die Partei". *Der Spiegel*, 41, October 5, 1981, pp. 193-196.

Fagivoli, Gianfranco, "Come a Fatima," *Domenica del Corriere*, September 1981, 2 installments, pp. 4-10 (with 12 photos), pp. 16-20; also in the first number of October, pp. 16-31.

Sabato (Milan): An important series of articles in the autumn, 1981.

Vesnič, M. "Bogorodica na mjestu sločina". ("The Mother of God at the scene of the crime") in *Novosti*, November 22, 1981. An article linking the apparitions with the events connected with the Ustaši.

Madre di Dio (Rome), November, 1981, February and March 1982, etc. Series of articles from a reliable source.

Notre Dame des Temps Nouveaux, 29, 1981, Number 6, November-December: a well documented article.

Laurentin, R., "La Vierge de Medjugorje", in *Le Figaro*, February 23, 1982: A preliminary report based on the information then available.

Goodnews (London), Numbers 44 to 47, February-April 1983.

Rooney L. and Faricy, R., "Notre Dame de la Paix: une relation sur les apparitions de la Vierge en Yougoslavie" in *Feu et Lumiere*, Number 1, October, 1983, pp. 22-27.

Madre, P., *Feu et Lumiere*, Number 2, November 1983, pp. 16-24.

Cassettes

Laurentin R., "La Vierge apparait-elle á Medjugorje?"

Madre P., "Á Medjugorje", ed. Diaconia, 41600 Nouans-le-Fuzelier.

Video-cassettes On Medjugorje And The Apparitions

The number increases each day. Recordings have been made in English, French, Italian, Portuguese.